MAP OF NORTH BORNEO

10 0

N

SULU
SEA

LABUK
BAY

SANDAKAN

NDAKAN
IDENCY

R. KINABATANGAN

R. SEGAMA

Tambisan

LAHAD DATU

DARVEL
BAY

TAWAU
RESIDENCY

SIBUTU

TAWAU

CELEBES SEA

CORAL IN THE SAND

CORAL
IN THE SAND

By

Geoffrey T. Bull

MOODY PRESS

CHICAGO

Printed in the United States of America

CONTENTS

Map of British North Borneo
see endpapers

PROLOGUE

No mention shall be made of coral
Or of pearls:
For the price of wisdom
Is above rubies.   Job

A sunlit strand along a South Sea island shore. Verdant jungle.
An azure sky. All around a scintillating sea. Land of a school-
boy's dreams. The only question, 'Where is the treasure?'
Suddenly we found it. Something white lay buried in the
gleaming sand. Carefully we dug. Deeper and deeper. Who
could have imagined it? Filigree beauty. Product of life; born
out of death. Slowly we lifted it, delicate branches pricking the
fingers. Matchless design forged in the deep. Washed in the sea,
we held it, splendid in the sunshine. Precious intricacy of God's
working in such distant waters. His pleasure woven into beauty.
Our great discovery, a labyrinth of coral in the sand.

Traced through these cameos from Borneo come flashes of
colour and glimpses of people. They represent a treasure-trove
of God's own coral, gleaned in that unfrequented island, where
the white-crested surf still breaks on benighted shores.

CHAPTER ONE

EASTWARD HO!

They shall fear the name of the Lord from the west,
And His glory from the rising of the sun.   Isaiah

SEVEN thousand feet over the China Sea and the twin-engined Dakota ploughed on, roaring its way into the breaking dawn. The sign of the tiger, fangs bared and ready for the prey, which adorned the fuselage, seemed a fitting symbol of this out-dated monster now leaping the waters between Singapore and Borneo.

By courtesy of the airlines and on account of delays on route, we were being allowed to travel first class on a tourist ticket. So apparently, were the *Straits Times* stacked in massive bundles on the seats in front of us. Candid and interesting 'fellow passengers' no doubt and sure of a warm welcome from news-hungry Europeans in Kuching and Jesselton but in the mean-while there was no prospect of conversation. I looked at the jumble of baggage and newspapers crudely lashed together and hoped against hope there would be no 'landslide' when at last the plane banked down out of the blue. Along the narrow corri-dor, the Malayan hostess glided to and fro, dexterously handing out trays of 'breakfast'. With my safety-belt unfastened and leaning forward, I could look through the swinging door at the end, right into the cockpit. A nostalgic feeling crept over me. It was reminiscent of those youthful days, when sitting behind the driver in a London bus, one would peep over his shoulder and try to gain a glimpse of the speedometer. What a for-midable set of instruments met my gaze! Trembling needles in round glassy eyes incessantly looked for the pilot's attention. To me these dials did at least give some atmosphere of technical security, but the handles in the floor were enough to shake the confidence of the most seasoned aeronaut. From time to time the pilot's hand would reach down frantically, give one or two of them a wrench, and leave the unofficial observer waiting for the worst. All too uncertain, I thought, and just imagine it, no more land for hundreds of miles! As I watched him, my admiration rose. It has always been a miracle to me how I ever co-ordinated my handbrake, clutch and accelerator to shed an 'L' plate on the ground and here was a man actually flying without an 'L' plate in the air! It was no good thinking too much about it. The plane was still flying in spite of everything. I turned from the cockpit and looked out of the window.

Far below a few needles of bare rock dotted the vast expanse. A film of haze hung over the water. Two or three hours passed slowly by. Then suddenly I was aware of an opaque tongue of land extending eerily towards us in the depths beneath. It was dark green, impressive and immense. It was the island of Borneo, the country which the Sulu natives still call 'The land below the Wind'.

There it lay. Vast stretches of steaming jungle lost in a back-drop of misty ranges clambering to the clouds. Meandering muddy rivers snaking their way down to the boundless sea. Long native huts standing in the clearings, and away to the far horizon, the ermine of a silver shore edging the soft texture of the rain forests. Fascinated beyond measure, I scrutinised the thrilling panorama. This then was the land of my fresh appoint-ment and my heart leapt out towards it, and its peoples. For a brief while my life and theirs would be inscrutably linked in the purposes of God.

To my shame I must confess a longstanding ignorance of things 'Bornean'. From my youth the word 'Borneo' always conjured up within my mind two rather terrifying ideas. One was that of wild uncontrollable woolly headed natives. The other was of completely uncontrollable orang-utans. Actually there are very few of either! How little is known of this colourful equatorial domain hanging like a jewel at the hems of Asia. As far back as seven hundred years ago Kublai Khan sent out his primitive commandos to prospect and invade the territory.

Some even identify the 'Seba' of the *Psalm for Solomon*[1] with the 'Sabah' used in the island to describe North Borneo today. In the sixteenth century intrepid Spanish and Portuguese mariners, navigated these almost legendary waters. From antiquity head-hunting tribes like the Dusuns and Muruts roamed the jungles stalking and killing animals and foes with their deadly blow-pipes. Along the coasts pirates marauded and plundered. Then late on the scene came British trade and eventually British rule. In the more settled conditions, Chinese communities began to flourish along the northern sea-board, head-hunting slackened and finally ceased. Gradually a semblance of order began to rise from the cruel strife-filled ages of the past and today the many peoples of Borneo go about their livelihood in peace.

The plane dipped low out of the skies and we touched down at Kuching, capital of Sarawak. This little town will, for the white man, always be a memorial of magnificence and misery. The era of the White Rajahs in the middle of the last century remains a fabulous memory but in that same place thousands of Australian, English and Dutch prisoners drank to the dregs a cup of filth, starvation, disease and murder, under the notorious and quixotic Japanese Colonel Suga. As we ran up the tarmac there was no more the groaning of the prisoner, nor did the stones cry out. It was just a sultry little airstrip, sun-baked and deserted in the silent and relentless heat. Our next stop was Sibu. How breathlessly still the airfields seemed. How great the sense of the un-real in such wide open spaces under the tropical sky. We did not land in the Sultanate of Brunei but flew over it. Below us the big silver oil drums were like newly minted sixpences strewn about the fields. The analogy is appropriate, for almost all the wealth of Borneo is gathered in the oil-fields there. By two o'clock we were landing on the island of Labuan. As we skimmed the tree-tops and came in close over the scrub we glimpsed a brief grassy stretch filled with tiny crosses. It was here the Japanese first landed in World War II and from here also that the invasion of North Borneo was launched in January

[1] Psalm 72, v. 10.

II

1942. The graves are the only reminder now. What must it have been to die in these out-reaches of the earth, flayed and bludgeoned under the sweltering sun; racked with malaria; lathered in the sweat of slave-labour; shot at the last and cast into a common grave. How many a heart in England and Australia today lies buried with the slain in this 'corner of a foreign field'. Before we left the 'old country' someone had asked us to find the grave of their boy. Maybe one of those little crosses belonged to him; but now the years have passed and through the blood-drenched land the rice and rubber grow again. The monsoon still blows through the bamboo, and men forget. They dig up bones no longer, as they plough the warm brown soil.

Three p.m. and the plane lunged in over extensive mangroves striding audaciously into the tide. A spic and span little airport raced to meet us. Government houses, slickly built in wood and asbestos flashed by the windows. Our tiger-decorated plane let out one final roar and then after a brief taxying-in, came to a reluctant halt. What a moment is journey's end! Great Britain to greater Borneo! No longer a world apart but just a day or two across the skies. Once through the customs, eager faces crowded around us, faces of Chinese men and women, changed by the power of Christ and jubilant in God. We could only clasp their hands and rejoice. The God who had sent us and now had brought us, was there to meet us. You could see Him shining in their eyes.

CHAPTER TWO

THE HOUSE OF THE GECKOS

The lizard . . . is in kings' palaces.   Agur

AFTER a few months in Borneo we all felt like old-timers. When we went shopping in Jesselton, where corrugated iron mingles with reinforced concrete, and joss sticks with transistor radios, we could pick out the new arrivals quite easily. How anæmic and unhealthy these Europeans looked just out from places like the U.K. How conspicuously white! We on the other hand having been first burnt red, peeled pink and finally 'skin-flaked', had been rewarded with a more respectable bronze tan. We felt a sense of merging, at least in some measure, with the more sallow skinned Dusuns and Chinese in the streets. People did not stop to stare at us, or whisper, "Look just out from England. I wonder which Government department he works in." Whatever length of time, however, one might live in Borneo, the first night is always unforgettable.

The meal was over and for a few minutes we were sitting in the cane chairs in the front room enjoying a respite from unpacking. We should, of course, have been talking to Mr. and Mrs. Pucknell, the missionaries we had come to relieve, but our eyes would wander unconsciously to the ceiling. To our astonishment it was alive with 'lizards'. "They are not lizards," explained Mr. Pucknell. "They are geckos. They have little suction pads on their feet and are great little fellows for catching mosquitoes. You'll get used to them." For my wife and myself it was simultaneously a spectacle of 'horror' and entertainment. There above our heads they scampered to and fro, grabbing flies, attacking moths, biting each others tails. Smack! Geckos fell in combat ten feet to the floor. Ke! Ke! Ke! Geckos called to each other across the room. Head-hunting and blow-pipes were not in it. Here was jungle warfare right on our door-step or rather on our roof-top. Life is never dull in the tropics. This was only the beginning. White beetles nearly the size of a plum and seemingly pilotless, would 'bringe' in, like V.2's, from the darkness, strike the boards and fall stunned to the floor. A praying mantis would creep up the mosquito proofing, a strange blend of the grotesque and the petite. Moths up to six inches in wingspan might flap in and flounder in the light. Gigantic scissor-grinding cicadas in black, yellow or green would cut the air and numb the ears. Perhaps the most menacing of all was the mosquitoes' guerilla warfare carried on at knee level. All else could be withstood but this attack more than anything would send you early to bed and to the shelter of your net. Gradually we were initiated to the means of counter attack. The main weapon is 'the coil'. These are bought in boxes, illustrated by a beautiful picture of a goldfish and inscribed with the Chinese characters *bao hsueh*, meaning 'blood protection'! Fixed to a little tin-stand and ignited, the coil burns like a circular stick of incense, sending off an aroma not unpleasant to humans but detestable beyond measure to mosquitoes.

Surviving the first evening we still had to survive the first night. The thing about the nights is that they are only hot whereas the days are hotter. At breakfast the thermometer greets you with a cheery eighty, lunch brings you into the nineties and then the temperature may not drop below eighty again until six p.m. The lowest temperature we ever recorded was 74° F. What makes life in Borneo a marathon endurance test, is not so much the intensity of heat but its continuance, coupled with an unremitting humidity. There are no seasons and therefore there is no relief. It is this sudden encounter with a climate of no escape which appalls the newcomer and makes the prospect of night formidable. After working all day in a bath of perspiration you lie beneath a mosquito net only to find after half an hour you are sleeping in a bath of perspiration, that is to say if you are sleeping. Then when all is dark the noises begin. Beetles burrow in the woodwork. Cats fight in the hollow roof, rats, if they dare, steal the soap and down will go an aluminium basin. The imperious chatter of the geckos sounds more insolent. Should it be raining the frogs strike up a symphony that lasts till dawn. If it is a feast day, sunrise is greeted with volley on volley of Chinese crackers. Sounds of dogs barking or an occasional cockcrow in the morn are minor items. The most eerie sound is probably the low 'humph-humph' of a giant toad croaking through the blackness of a night storm. By the time, however, our skins were sun-tanned we had become largely inured to these early adverse impressions and as the time goes on you wonder how it was that everything seemed so difficult at first.

Ross, aged four, and Peter, aged two, soon found that the best philosophy of life in Borneo, was to let their whole being get bound up in a bathing costume. From the beginning their energy astounded us. To them there seemed little difference between thirty-two and ninety-two degrees. Their motto seemed to be 'live every minute flat out to a finish'. As soon as breakfast was over they would want to go out to play. There were huge spiders that bit you till you bled, there were great black bees that stung you till you died, there were centipedes inches long, that could poison you beyond recall, not to speak of the millions of unseen bacteria armed for immediate attack. The children saw nothing and feared nothing; but we saw everything!

The house in which we lived was rented from a Cingalese, a genial fellow who could generally be relied upon to turn up at 8 a.m. on the very first day of the month for his rent. It had been standing now for about seven or eight years but was beginning to crumble, largely through the unceasing boring of insects in the timber. He had experts in one morning. "It is all right," they said, "the beetles are simply boring along the planks and not across into other planks." He was not consoled. When anything fell to bits we generally told him and he obligingly attended to it. High heels were out of the question for they went through the floor boards. We got along very well, probably because we did at least pay the rent which was not always so easily come by, further down the road. The house itself was wooden and built on concrete piles sunk into an old mangrove swamp. It was four feet off the ground. When the tide came up and the rains came down the waters met joyously ankle deep in the front garden. It was these conditions which were the delight of our two children, the neighbours' ducks, the countless frogs and one or two large land crabs which 'claimed' special burrowing rights on the premises. 'Under the house' was the 'heaven' of Ross and Peter, chiefly because there was plenty of sand and mud and also because it was the kind of place where irate parents would only penetrate if the situation was desperate. During drier periods, however, the garden had much to redeem it. The grass would be cut by a little wizened old man that looked like a Dusun but spoke Chinese. He would tootle round with his antiquated rotary-mower, surrounded with a blue haze of exhaust. It was wise to keep out of his way, as we soon found, when one day the mower hurled a piece of rock through one of the few glass windows as we sat at breakfast. There were quite a number of trees. Casuarinas,[1] a young coconut palm, numerous banana plantains and papayas. The first time we cut down a stalk of some eighty bananas I was duly photographed with the children, chopper in hand and incidentally, stains all over my shirt from the sap, which never came out.

One morning Peter came in weeping bitterly and pointed to his shoe. I pulled it off quickly and saw that one of his little toes was bleeding. As I was looking at it a yellow spider-like creature crawled from the shoe and slithered away into a crevice of the back stairs. It was one of those sickening moments when you hardly know what to do for the thought of what the incident might involve. My mind went back to Australia where we lived once, for a year, and I thought of the fatal funnel spiders and 'red backs'. I recalled reading in a Sydney newspaper of an 80 m.p.h. car dash for serum with a child suffering from a spider bite. Eighteen minutes from bite to injection and the child's life was saved. Were the spiders like that in Borneo? I had no

[1] Casuarinas: Tropical firs.

idea. What was it that had bitten him anyway? I could not tell. Quickly I picked him up in my arms, rushed him out of the front door and stepped straight into a friend's car which happened to be parked there that particular morning. I drove at once to the hospital and walked rather unceremoniously into the doctor's consulting room. The crowds of native folk waiting at the dispensary must have wondered whatever the dishevelled Englishman, clutching a dirty little boy, was wanting that morning. The doctor did not laugh at me but immediately gave Peter two injections and applied a dressing. As I drove home I could glimpse his little form hunched without movement on the back seat. Once indoors again, we put him down quietly on the bed. He was very subdued and lay still for a long time but after some hours he began to improve rapidly and all was well. It was our first scare. What a miracle of God that a car had been outside! It was the only morning since our arrival it had been there.

CHAPTER THREE

TRIAL BY FIRE

Nor was an hair of their head singed,
Neither were their coats changed.   Daniel

TANJONG ARU was an old location, which like many places in
Borneo since the war, had been enhanced by the erection of new
shop-houses. Built in the shape of a U, these buildings enclosed
the little market, and on any fine morning you might see a brisk
trade, as the local housewives and *amahs*[1] went to buy their
vegetables. There were two main corners, where the arms of the
U-shaped block turned to the main road, linking Jesselton with
the beach. These corners were occupied by coffee shops, one of
them being the Tanjong Aru Hotel, where moderate accommodation could be had, providing you could sleep through the
hurly-burly of the café below. Across the highway stretched
the spacious lawns, enclosures and grandstands of the Royal Turf
Club. Tanjong Aru village on race-days teemed with cars and
multiracial crowds. Stalls and primitive booths were erected,
and the shops hummed with business. Green coconuts, rich with
milk, were piled high ready for the thirsty racegoers, and the
policeman, especially appointed for the occasion, would mount
his little round box and direct the traffic in and out of the gates.
On the north side of the village was a Chinese Middle School,
where the boys would dash hither and thither, leaping and
shouting as they practised their basket-ball. Next to the school
was an open green, with clumps of palm trees lying well
back from the road, and once past the green you came to
a bumpy coral-track leading down towards the mangrove
swamps.

The first house in this side road was where we lived. You
could not miss it, because there was a notice board announcing,

[1] *Amah:* Malay for 'maidservant'.

in Chinese and English, that meetings were regularly held in the little preaching hall adjoining the house. A large text was always pinned on the board below, declaring in its own silent strength the best news of all. Thus rather ironically, it was gambling on one side of the street and preaching on the other! From our kitchen window on the race-days the horses and their colourful jockeys were clearly visible as they hurtled madly round the track and the very sound of their whips striking the horses' buttocks fell sharply on the ear. For our youngsters it was a grandstand view but presented somewhat of a dilemma for missionary parents! Such was Tanjong Aru, lashed by the tropical rains, baked in the noon-day sun, sleepy most of the time, noisy on occasions but still essentially pagan.

Behind the newer buildings and hidden from the main road lay another block of shop-houses. It had been hoped at one time to open a preaching place there in one of the premises but it was discovered that local regulations forbade such a procedure, and the idea was eventually dropped. In one of the upstair rooms, however, of these earlier-built shops, lived an ageing Chinese Christian and his family. They knew both the bitter and the sweet of life and had seen something of the heights and depths of human experience. At one time he had held an important government post on the Chinese mainland and had done much in his hey-day to help his fellow-countrymen. A man of ability and æsthetic taste, he and his family had lived in a commodious house set in its own grounds. He had enjoyed very real authority, commanding his own private soldiers and being escorted by a personal bodyguard as he moved about his home-town reorganising the life of the community following the ravages of war. The time came, however, when his immediate superior fell into disfavour with the higher authorities and he was compelled, unexpectedly, to leave for Canton. Later, when the Communist armies marched into South China, the whole family came to Hong Kong and almost everything was lost. After much difficulty they had managed to emigrate to North Borneo. Thus it was that they were now living in these humble quarters in

Tanjong Aru. Ta-Ko,[1] the only son in the family, was now at high school, whilst his father had succeeded in obtaining a post in the local Middle School, as a teacher of Chinese. Ta-Ko was a very promising boy. Although he could but dimly remember the former prosperous days, he had, nevertheless inherited his father's abilities if not his substance, and was now doing well at his lessons. His father had great hopes of him, but of all things that Ta-Ko had done of late, the best undoubtedly was this. He had put his trust in the Lord Jesus Christ as His Saviour. He had taken his stand as a real Christian. That was in the year 1956 . . .

. . . Suddenly I woke up and gazed intently through the mesh of the mosquito-net to the glassless window, and through the window, out into the night beyond. Something was wrong. The sky was not as black as it ought to be. It could hardly be more than 1 a.m. Whatever was happening with the sky? In a flash I had bounded out of the room to the front of the house and opened the door. I stood aghast.

How incredibly reminiscent of that moment, when in 1941 I had opened the front door in my old home in a north west suburb of London. Father was an air-raid warden and at the sound of the siren had just rushed out into the darkness to report for duty. Then the bombs had fallen, a long string of them, right across our district. The lights went out; the glass came in; and the embers of the fire jumped into the hearth. Then it was that I had opened the door only to be choked and blinded with dust, but not before I had glimpsed through the rubble-laden air the terrifying glare of a vast inferno belching upward over the roof-tops of the factories just below. The whole sky was full of flaming light. As I stood at the doorway that night in Tanjong Aru, that dreadful war-time scene was re-enacted before my eyes. The fire appeared so great and so near, that I felt we should have to evacuate the house almost immediately. I hastily called brother Pucknell who at that time had not yet left for

---

[1] Ta-Ko: Romanised Chinese for 'Big Brother'.

Australia. A few moments and he was out of bed, standing with me on the front steps. Together we looked across to the old shop-houses. Grasping the direction, he suddenly cried, "Quickly—that's where some of the Christians live!" There was hardly a moment to don any extra clothes, so we just sped out along the main road, past the race-course; on past the Middle School, towards the village. It was like daylight. The spectacle was fearful beyond description and a withering heat surged through the air. As we drew near I could see a ragged sheet of flame, blood-yellow, lunging madly forward from shop to shop and house to house. In quick succession each dwelling was enveloped until the entire block of buildings, housing some three hundred souls, was totally engulfed. People—Chinese, Malays and Indians—stood helplessly about in groups, eyes glassy with dread, reflecting the eerie light of the fire. One man not far from the Tanjong Aru Hotel seemed quite demented. He was jumping incessantly up and down on the pavement in a frenzy of grief and rage, utterly frantic in his unspeakable distress. Long serpent tongues of fire, multi-forked, shot out venomously into the night sky instilling silent terror into the hearts of every spectator. Unbeknown to us, four children were struggling for their lives, trapped in their rooms somewhere in that raging cauldron of heat. Grown-ups, too, were suffocating in the dense fumes, striving to reach the pavement but falling in the passage ways, caught in the scorching air and burned to death.

All at once on the little grass patch by the fruit-market, we caught sight of Ta-Ko and his family. They were safe. At his feet was a sheet tied in a big knot at the corners. Inside the bundle was all he had left in the world.

Only two or three days previously they had all been so delighted when the new piano had arrived. It had been quite an acquisition for the whole family, and Ta-Ko had dreams, perhaps, of having his young Christian friends to sing hymns and choruses around it there in his home. The living-room had also been enlarged recently and things were beginning to look up again after the hard times of recent years. "You had better insure the piano," his father had counselled, but no one felt disposed to make the effort and take the journey specially into town. It could be done another day. It would not matter very much. So eventually they had retired to bed. In the middle of the night Ta-Ko awoke. He sniffed the air. There was undoubtedly a smell of burning. Since he had been living in Tanjong Aru there had been several alarms and he was immediately on the alert. Tip-toeing downstairs he opened the door and looked out onto the dark and deserted street. Then to his consternation he perceived an orange glow was shining through the upstairs window of the house, next door but one. As he listened he could hear the crackle of flames and then, as he continued watching, he caught his first sight of the fire. Out from one of the upstairs windows clambered the barber, whom he knew quite well. Although the man was moving as fast as he could, he was obviously still acting with great care. As he stepped onto the broad parapet overhanging the street, Ta-Ko could see he had one of his little children in his arms. In a moment Ta-Ko turned and with giant strides leapt up the stairway and woke the family. As the news of the fire was shouted up and down the block, pandemonium broke loose. Who could tell how fast the fire might spread? There might be a lee-way of no more than five minutes then all would be lost. On the table in the living-room lay a pile of paintings belonging to his father. Some dated back as far as the fifteenth century and had recently been exhibited in Jesselton. Ta-Ko snatched as many as he could and would have taken these to safety but some fell and bounced roughly down the stairs. There were two typewriters. They ought to go, and clothes of course, not to speak of his precious books. Smoke began to fill the house. Then the lights failed. Obviously the flames had reached next door because the neighbours came walking along the parapet and started climbing through the windows of the room. All was confusion. They could only bundle up a few things in a sheet and go. Hurriedly and sadly they clattered down the stairs for the last time. The street was lined with people standing amidst their furniture, pots and pans, and all sorts of bits and pieces

22

connected with their tiny homes. Floors and roofs were beginning to cave in and the crowds were being forced back and back from the flames. Ta-Ko and his family moved slowly over to the green. As they looked behind them, their living-room was already a mass of flames. They had been just in time.

As we stood with them in the fearful glow of the fire I said to Ta-Ko, "Come on, let me carry your bundle and we can put you all up in the Gospel Hall tonight." With a big jerk of my shoulder I humped it up onto my back and with face bent down towards the ground I marched off along the road. I could not see if any of them were following me. Apparently they were loath to leave the scene of tragedy, so they lingered still, watching the blaze die down until it was no more than a sullen heap of red exploding cinder.

In a lather of perspiration I lowered my heavy load onto the floor of the little preaching chapel adjoining our house and wondered what had become of Ta-Ko. An hour must have passed and my wife and I decided to return to bed. Then, at about 2.30 a.m., the sound of footsteps came crunching up from the road and we knew that Ta-Ko had come. There he stood in the half-light, a fine young man, quietened and subdued after the ordeal of the night, but not dismayed. I led him into the little hall and switched on the electric light. The geckos and cockroaches scampered away and the big black Chinese characters, written by Ta-Ko's father, stood out over the rostrum. "Believe," they said, "and thou shalt be saved." We turned to the bundle and Ta-Ko began to pore over its contents, turning back the clothes and oddments, and diligently searching for something that was obviously very valuable to him. I wondered what he had lost. Could it be money, a photograph, some personal documents perhaps, which he hoped against hope, had not been burned. Suddenly his hidden thought found expression. "Where is my Bible?" he said. . . .

"Where is my Bible?" Here was gold coming through the fire. Here was one of Christ's men in Borneo, a young believer,

23

standing in the night, undaunted by hazard or adversity. I watched him, as he calmly moved and quietly spoke, deeply conscious of the harrowing hours through which he had just passed. "Where is my Bible?" Behind him now lay nothing but the charred remains of his erstwhile home, yet he was held by the Truth which stands for ever. No gold like the Book, no treasure like the everlasting Word! Ta-Ko's values were gloriously unimpaired.

Just seven and a half hours later at 9 a.m. on the following morning, the young people began to gather for their usual Bible Class. Although he had been up all night, Ta-Ko was there. In opening the service I invited someone to choose a 'chorus'. It was Ta-Ko who first spoke. We turned to the number and the little harmonium struck up cheerily. What was his choice? The words were these:

> "Jesus, Thou art everything to me
>   All my lasting joys are found in Thee
> Jesus, Thou art everything to me."

Joyfully the witness winged its way across the open green and through the palms to the blackened shell of old Tanjong Aru.

Ta-Ko was amongst the undefeated. His was a faith 'obtaining the promises' and 'quenching the violence of fire'.

CHAPTER FOUR

DRAGONS AND THE ISLAND

Let them give glory unto the Lord,
And declare His praise in the islands. Isaiah

It was New Year time and the mask fell off. Jesselton, capital of British North Borneo with its blocks of flats and shops, its thriving little harbour, where they unload a ship a day, and its shiny new cars, suddenly lost its veneer of sophistication. The 'dragons' came out on to the street. Every morning we had been accustomed round about seven o'clock, to hearing a stream of traffic go by on the main road outside. There went the latest limousines of the west and the oldest bone-shakers of the east, bundling in the sleepers of the suburbs to become the down-town workers of the day. Between the airport and the wharf, on a thin coastal strip some four miles long, lived about twenty thousand people. There were turbaned Sikhs, Cingalese, Indians, Malays and colourfully attired natives from the hinterland. The town's population, however, was about 90 per cent Chinese and their age-old culture with the influx of modern amenities gave the cosmopolitan community a distinct air of civilisation. But then the 'dragons' came, and there was the re-enactment of those same sinister devilish dances that characterise the country towns of China. Down all the millenniums of the royal dynasties, China's national emblem has been the dragon. The Emperor's Throne boasted itself as the Dragon Throne and the entire religious life of the country was stamped with the mark of the dragon and its temples. Today the dragon may be red in colour but its flaming fangs still devour and ravage China's millions from old Peking's palaces. In Borneo the dragon (make no mistake) still deceives. To the sound of a million crackers that covered the streets in decimated scraps of red paper, the dragon processions marched out. Artistry was sadly lacking. In China

25

the 'dragon' assembles at evening time. Every man composing it, carries a lantern and the thin thread of light, crowned by the dragons-head in bamboo and coloured paper, meanders through the crowds, who watch with growing fascination. In Jesselton, rattling lorries, full of young people belabouring gongs, toured the town visiting the homes of the devotees of Buddhism. On arrival all would dismount, the laughable crude head of a gigantic dragon be donned and between them a dance would be performed. Yet the old movements and satanic sense would come back as they pranced and bowed before the door. For all its twentieth-century burlesque [1] it is still the emblem of the Evil One and his ancient grasp remains as cruel and firm. As they shot past our house and the Christians' meeting hall, the gongs and drums were beaten harder. There seemed a special note of defiance and arrogance. We were glad to see that they went past Mrs. Su's house opposite. She used to worship the moon but now she belongs to Christ. The dragon did not stop. He had been defeated there. Other houses gladly received the motley deputation. The old lady on the other side rose early and burned her joss-sticks in the garden. She made a fire of paper as an offering and bowed with her hands in entreaty to the unseen demons. Her face was hard and fixed. After her devotions she returned into her up-to-date bungalow equipped with every modern convenience. As the old mother-in-law, she no doubt ruled the household and it was easy to understand how the younger members of the family did not turn to the Lord we preached. For days it was bedlam, with gongs, dragons and crackers everywhere. Europeans smiled benignly at these childish Chinese charades. The boys and girls had a great time playing at dragons and even Ross and Peter wanted a cardboard box, with a hole in the bottom to put over their heads to do the same. What, however, is the moral background to these ludicrous yet pernicious remnants of superstition? The following incident is indicative.

One January not far off from the Chinese New Year festivities

[1] Some 'dragons' are organised by students collecting for charities.

a high government official, acting no doubt on certain information that had come to his knowledge, carried out a surprise raid on a heathen temple in North Borneo. As he expected, he found a large number of persons gambling. Charges were made and heavy fines imposed on the offenders. The devotees of the temple were furious and special measures were taken, it was alleged, to bring about a revenge for what they considered was an impious intrusion. Day and night the candles burned before the demons. The aroma of incense filled the place. The entreaty went on incessantly. Would not the 'deities' wreak vengeance on their enemies? A few weeks later the official stepped into a Shackleton aircraft and the plane soared up over the jungles and out over the west coast. He was scanning the waters for pirate ships that still operate at times amongst the islands and along the remoter shores. Suddenly and quite unaccountably, the plane plunged into the sea. The green waters filled the cabin. No boats were at hand to rescue. All perished. The mystery is still unexplained. Can demons toss an aeroplane into the sea? God knows. What is certain, however, is that behind the façade of refrigerators, air-conditioners, electric fans and all the array of western attractions flooding the newly built stores, there still leers the face of a real, personal immoral devil that is determined to bind the people and resist the on-march of the liberating Gospel of Christ.

During the Chinese New Year period, all Jesselton was on holiday for several days. What could be better than for all the young people of the church to have a day together! "Let's go to the islands," they all said. For some of the younger ones this probably conjured up a youthful paradise of eating curry puffs and ice-cream under the palm trees but there was more to be thought of than that. "What about a boat?" we asked.

"I'll fix up a boat," said Chang-Shen.[1]

"Who'll do the organising?"

"Oh, leave that to Te-P'ing."[2]

Before we knew what was happening, the 'voyage' was on.

[1] Mighty Victory. [2] Virtuous Peace: Chinese masculine names.

We decided that everybody should meet at the wharf at 8 a.m. the following Friday. With typical western punctuality our family were on parade at that early hour, ready for the desert-island trip. To our chagrin not a soul was in sight and certainly no boat drawn alongside, for the tide was out. By about nine everybody had arrived. Apparently we were still uninitiated to Borneo's perpetual 'summer-time'! "Where is the boat?" we said. Somebody pointed towards a thin channel of deep water opposite the fruit-market. There it was, a ramshackle pale-blue launch lying at anchor in the mud. As I looked at its wide bottom I felt somewhat reassured. There were no sharks inshore we had been told, but I was glad to feel that the possibility of capsizing, with all these precious young lives aboard, was not so likely. A few minutes' walk brought us opposite the launch, only to find there was about one hundred yards of slime, mud, old tyres, broken bottles and other rubbish from the market to be negotiated, before we could clamber on board. Further, the descent from the high sea wall on to these un-inviting flats was by means of a broken wooden ladder with only three rungs in the drop of some eight feet. This was nothing to the youthful members of the party but to the not-quite-so-young mother of one of the girls it was almost insurmountable. She was lowered valiantly, albeit unceremoniously, rather like some ballast down on to the beach by the wiry young Chinese arms. Once on board and with all the picnic gear piled on the decks, we were set for the day. A grey bank of cloud still held the sun at bay, so as yet it was comparatively cool. We nosed our way out past the cairns of rugged coral that marked the channel, and threading our way through the reefs, headed out to sea. It was a cheery band singing, chatting and laughing. Behind us the waterfront of Jesselton stretched out in a long thin line, the new architecture of the banks and shops gradually giving way to more primitive native huts in the old *kampongs*[1] amongst the palms and the mangroves. Away southward we could see Tanjong Aru Point close to where our house was situated. High

[1] *Kampong:* Malay for 'village'.

28

over the town on the cliff tops were the 'million dollar flats', magnificent tenements built for the more privileged of government servants.

After some time out, we sailed on the lee-side of Gaya Island. It was thickly wooded and the only signs of life were some timber cuttings on the low hills and fishermen's huts standing on poles just offshore. There was no sign of the old town of Gaya, the original Jesselton of North Borneo. The story goes that in the days of the expansion of the Chartered Company by which North Borneo was originally developed and administrated for the British, the young relatives of the Sultans became angered at the threat to their birthright. Amongst these was an adventurous and ambitious young man called Mat Salleh. He had entered the family circle of the Sultan of Sulu by marriage and very soon became the champion of the lost cause. One night a conspiracy came to fruition. Gaya was attacked and the original town burned to the ground by the insurgents. The responsible British official of that time was murdered on a hill just behind the smouldering ruins, and a war began which lasted many years in different parts of the territory. The conflict only came to an end when at Tambunan in the interior of Borneo, Mat Salleh was accidentally killed by a bullet from one of his own guns fired from his fort a mile or so away. After this, the town of Gaya was moved to the main island and rebuilt under the Malay name of *Api-Api* which means 'fire-town'. And this is the name commonly used by both Chinese and Malays for Jesselton today.[1]

As we rounded Gaya Island on the south side, another small island hove in sight. It was reminiscent of those pictures that illustrate Stevenson's *Treasure Island* and which have stirred the imaginations of schoolboys for generations. Deep down in the crystal waters lay the coral reefs. As we drew nearer we could see there was just one sandy beach on which to land, with the jungle coming right down to the shore. The island was about a quarter of a mile long, rising to perhaps eighty feet in the centre,

[1] The Chinese adaption of the Malay, being 'Ya-Pi'.

where a tall palm protruded above the dense mass of the other trees. The launch came in close to land, where the bottom shelved very steeply to great depth. One by one we jumped ashore and gradually began to spread out, exploring and scavenging for shells. There was not a living soul to be seen. The stillness and the beauty were breathtaking and the waters cool to the feet, whereas on the mainland the water is often too warm for enjoyable paddling. We found a big tree shading the beach and chose this spot for the picnic, whilst one party decided to go right round the island clambering over the rocks hunting for whatever 'treasures' they might find. Because these islands are little visited it is possible to find shells and coral of rare beauty. It was here too, we first saw living coral and felt its soft slippery touch underfoot. After an hour or two, folk began to wander back to the big tree exhausted through trekking in the heat, for the sun was out now in its full strength. Some had been boating in the little canoe from the launch and others swimming. During the day some of the fellows decided to rig up a kind of Bajau[1] craft out of the canoe. Tee-Ay was the leader. He was of the aristocracy of Malaya and had been brought up as a Moslem. Later, however, he had, with great courage, turned from that dark and fanatical religion to yield his life to Christ. There was a quiet radiance and strength in his face. It had cost him everything to publicly confess Jesus as Lord. Now he was teaching in Jesselton and was at his best today, having fun with the youngsters. A Bajau boat is a boat used by the Bajau natives. Its distinctive feature is one large square sail which is hoisted in a diamond shape upon a single mast. From somewhere, a light blanket or piece of canvas had been discovered and over the narrow canoe, with the help of slender looking sticks, it was now hoisted in true Bajau style. It was a long laborious process in the hot sun but at last, Tee-Ay lay low and still in the bottom of the canoe, valiantly endeavouring to control his Bajau sail. Slowly he was pushed off into deeper water and the equilibrium of the vessel amazed us. "Well done, Tee-Ay!" But Tee-Ay was not

[1] *Bajau:* the name of a Borneo tribe.

30

a Bajau and the sail would not do what a Bajau could make it do. Slowly the canoe began to heel over, then gaining momentum disgorged her 'cargo' into the coral sea. Tee-Ay, looking more like a drowned rat than a 'prince', emerged with a huge grin, stretching from ear to ear.

"Dinner ready!" Everybody was ready for it too. Chang-Shen stood as president over a large pot of curried chicken, which was doled out into a veritable assortment of bowls and dishes. There was no water on the island but nothing had been forgotten, bottles of 'cold boiled water', *leng k'ai shui*, as the Chinese say, had been provided in abundance and even the ice-cream dream was realised. The youthful organisation had not failed!

As the curried chicken and ice-cream diminished, folk quietened down and after a little while a number of us went over to a big log and sat on it with our backs to the jungle and with our eyes looking out across the lovely straits to Gaya. Then someone began to sing, not just any song but a song that echoed from the very hearts of these young people snatched from a cess-pool of superstition by the saving power of Christ. As we joined in, the melody rang out in that exquisite setting with a joy which finds its spring in God . . .

> "Wonderful grace of Jesus,
>   Greater than all my sin;
>   How shall my tongue describe it,
>   Where shall its praise begin?
>   Taking away my burden,
>   Setting my spirit free,
>   For the wonderful grace of Jesus
>   Reaches me."

As the sun began to go down in the afternoon sky we packed up our bits and pieces. It had been good to leave the 'dragons' behind for a day and renew ourselves in mind and body. We would go back stronger for the fight on the mainland.

Slowly the little launch drew away from the coral strand and a wind began to whip the calm sea into angry waves. It was getting stormy.

"Look," said somebody, and all eyes were strained for a last moment, at the deserted beach. They were right. The monkeys were coming out of the jungle and down to the shore.

CHAPTER FIVE

FISHING FROM THE WINDOW

Canst thou draw out leviathan with a hook?
Or his tongue with a cord which thou lettest down?   Job

THE sun had just dipped beyond the islands, leaving a memory of gold in the soft grey sky. Low on the horizon the night clouds were marshalling their chariots of cumulus, eager to possess the abdicated heaven. How the serenity of the eastern night bewitches the squalor of the tropics! Dirt merges into the darkness and tired eyes look up to the stars. The dust and heat relent, a soft breeze comes gently in from the sea and the palm trees stand in beauty, the last proud sentinels of a dying day.

As I walked towards the tumbledown shelter, the ground was still wet underfoot. The monsoon was breaking and the recent torrential rain had left large muddy puddles lying across the path. As the light faded each one became a placid mirror of the infinite above. What a parable of clay and glory! There is something after all to say for puddles, and for men too, if they bring the splendour of the heavens into our common way.

I found the narrow causeway, built of broken coral, brushed past the big oil drum serving as a water butt and approached the front door. At the edge of the coral was a small assortment of cut-down kerosene tins. Flowers were bravely struggling up-wards from the meagre soil. The front door was virtually non-existent, the entrance being a communal doorway into a long wooden hut built on piles out over the water. I walked in, and at the sound of my none-too-gentle footsteps on the bare floor-boards, a bright-faced Chinese boy looked up and greeted me. He motioned me to a door which led into Ko-Ko's[1] quarters. I stood for a moment waiting for it to open. What a poor kind of place for a home, I thought. Over in one corner was an old

[1] Ko-Ko: Romanised Chinese for Older Brother.

bicycle and a big earthen pot. On the opposite side was a bamboo cradle and a crude table attended by one or two chairs. A corridor led away into darkness and the sounds of people. "Come in," said Ko-Ko cheerily, and with a broad smile he welcomed me to his bachelor 'den'. He was a Hakka Chinese, and stood little more than five feet in height, with jet black hair crowning his eager young face. His eyes were black too, but bright and penetrating. I noticed one was a little bloodshot. He had been fighting blindness for years. Rather than sit down in the closeness of the room we walked over to the window, and pushing back the net-curtain, leant together on the sill, looking out into the night. It was completely dark now and the tide was just beginning to ebb. We could perceive the outflow of the water between the houses perched upon their piles. Linking these precarious dwellings was a warren of slatted timber runways. Over these inshore waters countless families live and die. Only their employment, shopping, or maybe some personal excursion, will take them on to the dry land. "Don't the children get drowned sometimes?" I asked once. "Yes, sometimes," had been the casual answer. We did not say much at first. There was something restful in just looking into the darkness after the glare and work of the day. Here and there a light from a window would send down a tremulous finger into the murky depths below. A woman busied herself on a verandah near at hand. There was the sound of continuously dripping water mingled with the incessant twitter of innumerable swallows nesting beneath the houses. Away on the mainland the car lights picked out the coast road into Jesselton.

"How's the fishing been going lately?" I suddenly asked Ko-Ko.

"Haven't done any for some time," he said, although obviously quite glad to talk about it.

"What's your method when you do it?"

"Oh, it's very simple," he said, "I sit here at my table studying, and keep the line dangling out of the window. I generally use meat for bait. With just occasional interruptions to pull in the fish, you can keep on reading, yet still catch quite a cheap supper at the same time."

I must say I personally had never found fishing quite so straight-forward as that but the idea intrigued me.

"What sort of fish do you catch?" I ventured to ask. Ko-Ko seemed to lose something of his amateur air as he began now to take up the subject.

"Well," he continued, "there are first-class fish and there are fourth-class fish. The first-class are really a kind of mullet. It is not so easy to catch those but the fourth-class are no trouble to pull in. The only thing is that they have horns and are poisonous. The biggest one I ever caught," he said, holding his hands some twelve inches apart, "was about this size.

"More recently," he went on, "when I have caught fish I have been giving them to the neighbours." Ko-Ko was obviously sincere but I could only hope that the ones he had caught recently, were really 'first-class'!

We turned back from the window, dazzled by the electric light. This was the sole modern amenity and was undoubtedly the outstanding factor in making such a shack habitable. I looked about the room. It was without question a bachelor apartment, the chief indulgence being that things had been allowed to stay just where Ko-Ko had left them! On a line stretched between two nails across one corner, was a heterogeneous display of damp washing awaiting the sea breezes. An empty crate stood on end, serving as a washstand. A bucket and a kettle nestled close together on a low kerosene stove. A camp bed, a desk and a couple of old chairs completed the furniture. White paper had been pasted on the wooden walls, more, perhaps, to keep out the draughts than for adornment but the floor was still bare.

"This is the best place I have had since I left home," said Ko-Ko, sensing my scrutiny. I could well believe it. His room was one of seven, crouching under that corrugated iron roof. Six families shared the building, each family occupying one of the other rooms. How relative wealth is. As a young clerk working in a local bank, and enjoying one whole room to himself, his position would be viewed by other tenants as fabulous.

We sat down at the desk and began to talk. Of course there was the usual conglomeration of odds and ends lying about. Pens, pencils, scissors, some medicine and a few treasured photos, one perhaps more treasured than the others, who knows? There were books, even a little portable radio, and a calendar or two. A few old Christmas cards hung here and there on the wall, and broke in some degree, the sense of austerity. But there was something else on the wall. Something that gave meaning to the unconscious happiness that Ko-Ko exhibited in those threadbare surroundings. The words were written on a card and I looked at them thoughtfully.

> "I live yet not I . . .
> Christ liveth in me."[1]

Dwelling on that simple statement the bare room in the little shack over the waters at Jesselton fades for a moment. The years slip back. There is another little room looking out maybe on to the estuary of the Tiber. The most civilised article is the quill that Paul holds. Maybe, too, there is just a rough table, a few personal things and some washing drying on a line. He is writing to some of his friends away in Galatia. What shall I tell them from this bare prison cell? He knows what to tell them.

> "I live yet not I . . .
> Christ liveth in me."

Almost twenty centuries between Italy of yesterday and Borneo of today. But the secret has been passed on. That was why I had come to Borneo, to do just that. I looked at Ko-Ko across the desk. There he sat with his elbows resting on the plastic floral tablecloth. How did the miracle happen to him? A few days earlier I had been talking to a mutual acquaintance in an electrical shop in town. "Have you noticed something about Ko-Ko," I said. "Yes, I have," he replied, without hesitation.

[1] Galatians 2, v. 20.

I was determined to find out for myself tonight, the story that lay behind his transformed life . . .

"It was over forty years ago," began Ko-Ko, "that my father came to Borneo." As he mentioned his father, my mind went back automatically to my meeting with him. He was a short little Chinese gentleman, more cultured than the first impression might allow, and possessed of a surprising command of English. "Of course, he is retired now," continued Ko-Ko, "but all the time he has been here he has been employed on the railway staff as a clerk. The first home I can remember was situated just below the clock tower and my earliest recollections are of its chimes awaking me each morning. Down at the foot of the hill, there ran the railway line and there you could see the original Jesselton station which has long since been demolished. Daddy being on the railway, we didn't do too badly for food, and we used to get our rice regularly and nearly always some vegetables or even fish and eggs with it. We had an old dog too, I remember him. *Tai Meng* we called him. It means 'too mad' but for all that, he still died of old age. In those days before the last war we didn't go to school and anyway, when I was only seven, the Japs came in. A big fleet of ships brought them here. They didn't have to fight although I remember seeing some smoke rising from the direction of the wharf. Something must have been set on fire. They marched into town and some went out as far as 'Mile Three'. They had brown uniforms and wore caps. Sturdy little men they were. Not long after, the rationing started and each family received an allotment of food according to the number of children they had.

"My lasting impression of those days though, was the night of the 'Double Tenth' 1943. That evening I was staying out at my granny's place, some two and a half miles from Jesselton. She lived amongst the trees on the top of a ridge of hills."

Knowing the district I could picture where he meant.

"My uncle and his family lived there too. It was a place where they used to grow pineapples, and I often went out there to see my cousins. Suddenly in the middle of the night my grand-mother woke us all up. Something terrible was happening. We could hear the machine-gun fire rattling away somewhere in the valley below. . . ."

Naturally Ko-Ko was too young at that time to understand what was happening, but the occasion of which he spoke was that fateful evening when the people of Jesselton and the surrounding district rose up against their Japanese oppressors. They were led by a Dr. Kok who with other leaders had organised a for-midable resistance known as the 'Kinabalu Guerrillas'. As night came on they began to gather in the region of Mengattal, a village situated amongst the rubber plantations some ten miles out of town. Shadowy forms mustered secretly and silently amongst the trees and then by a pre-arrangement, the guerrillas moved in towards Jesselton by truck or on foot. By means of underground liaison with the natives on some of the offshore islands it was possible under the cover of darkness, for the native boats filled with men, to creep in close to the sea wall. At a given moment the two forces combined and in one swift battle succeeded in capturing the Jesselton armoury. The defending Japanese forces were killed and as many as sixty of them be-headed in the town and up through the villages towards Kota Belud. The oppressed people thus erupted in vengeance and bloodshed and the rebellion continued in different parts of the colony until the Allied landings and liberation, eighteen months later. The Japanese reprisals were appalling. Two thousand of the local inhabitants were put to death. Cruel tortures were inflicted upon many innocent victims. A reign of terror began.

Ko-Ko resumed his story.

"As we listened fearfully to the machine-gun fire, my grand-mother and uncle discussed what would be the best thing to do. To wait till the whole area was purged by the Japanese was useless. We children needed to be taken away, so my uncle looked at us all and then chose two of my cousins along with myself. He got out his bicycle and together we began to descend the hill, creeping down the little paths and through the under-

growth to the road that lead back inland to Inanam and Mengattal. It was a hazardous undertaking—a man and three young
children racing against time. We hoped to get well into the
interior before Japanese reinforcements overran the whole
district, for we feared they would just shoot and kill all in
their path. On we went, taking turns to sit on the bicycle, for
our little legs tired easily as we trudged on mile after mile.
Through the rice fields we passed and then after a long while,
we cut up through rubber trees along a little track known to my
uncle. It was dark and eerie through the trees and we seemed to
go on for an interminable distance. Then ahead we could see
something burning. What could it be? There was a river to
cross before we could get to the little hamlet where we had
relatives. If we could only get there before daybreak we would
have some measure of safety. As we broke out of the trees, to
our horror the wooden bridge was in flames. My poor uncle
was in a dilemma. No doubt the local people were burning it
down for the defence of their village against the inevitable
counter-attacks of the Japanese. Meanwhile we were stranded
in the jungle. As we approached the bridge we could see there
was just a small width of wood left between the flames. The
heat and smoke were terrific. 'Run through! Run through!'
shouted my uncle, and on we ran. The last memory I have of
my uncle that early morning hour was seeing him pick up his
bike and return in the direction of my grandmother's home.
We children had been instructed what to do, so once over the
bridge we went without delay to our relatives' home. We were
sad to hear later on that my brave uncle was caught soon afterwards by the Japanese and thrown into prison. Life in the little
jungle village was hectic. As we expected, the Japanese soon
caught up with us and began to maraud the district. They would
come storming into the village, shooting at sight and it wasn't
long before we learned how to hide. Soon we had built a little
shelter far away in the dense forest and although we often used
to creep back to the village at night, we were always back
in the jungle by dawn. In the midst of all the suffering and

39

bloodshed God cared for me but like most youngsters I never thought of Him then."

"What happened next?" I asked.

"Oh, things quietened down after a while. The Japanese cut down on the shooting and I was able to come back to my own home in Jesselton. In the end it was even possible for my uncle to receive food in prison. In 1945 when the war, unbeknown to us, was almost finished, our whole family moved up to Tenom and we planted rice and maize. Things took a definite turn for the better. There was a Japanese camp nearby and we were able to barter bananas for quinine, which was a great help. One day when I was up at the camp I noticed that the Camp Commandant looked very disturbed. He was saying something to his fellow-officers which I could not understand. Afterwards I found out that the Japanese had lost the war and that all their forces in Borneo must surrender. After that, hundreds and hundreds came marching down from Keningau on their way to Jesselton. For a long time my father had been down there, but we had never heard from him and I was so sad because it was very easy to get shot by the Japanese. In fact it was during that period that I first prayed and I used to cry sometimes just thinking of the possibility of his being killed. I remembered how my old granny used to say there was a 'heavenly Father', and how she used to give thanks for her food."

"Did you not go to school all that time?"

"No, I didn't go to school until I was eleven. Then, of course, it was hard to make up for lost time. One of the things I first remember learning though, was a kind of catechism, which began:

> 'Who made you?
> God made me.
> Why did God make you?
> That I may glorify Him!'

but I liked playing marbles and chess mostly and the drill and football were the greatest fun to me. To be quite honest, it was during those teenage years that I began to go to pieces. We had all been through a lot and now that peace had come I guess we didn't know how to enjoy it. Daddy began to drink and when he came home he would quarrel with mummy. He joined a club in town, and life became just one big gamble of cards and mah-jong. My home and family which had pulled through the war began to break up now. I didn't help matters either. I followed my father, ganged up with rough company and started on the gambling run too. Needless to say, I failed my exams time and again. Drink brought my dear parents to the brink of divorce. The little security I had known seemed about to fall through altogether. I began to know what it meant to be thoroughly miserable."

I listened sympathetically and as he began to hesitate, I urged him to continue.

"About that time," he resumed, "I was feeling particularly fed up one evening. There wasn't a single fresh thing to do so I decided to go and see my old partner in 'crime', P'eng-Yu.[1] He was one of the wildest boys at school, and although he had seemed a bit different of late we still got on fine. Perhaps we could scrape together enough, I thought, to get out to the cinema. I jumped on my bike and quite soon had reached his house. It was one of the few two-storey buildings in the district, with a coral causeway entrance.

"You may know it," he said, "it's not far from here."

"Well, I parked the cycle and went up to the entrance of the house. I could tell something was going on inside. It sounded like people singing. As it happened there was a whole crowd there, so I just walked in. To my amazement there was an Englishman standing up in front of everybody. He had a whole room full of people listening to him and he was writing on a blackboard. What staggered me was that he was speaking fluent Chinese. Whatever had gone wrong with P'eng-Yu and his family I couldn't imagine. 'I suppose the cinema is out any-way,' I thought, glancing round. Then I suddenly realised the

[1] P'eng-Yu: Romanised Chinese for 'friend'.

foreigner was speaking about Jesus Christ. As I listened I was unaccountably drawn into the circle. The things he was saying I had never heard before. Was he making it up or could it really be true what he was saying about Jesus? I looked casually towards the end of the bench on which I was sitting and caught sight of an elderly English lady. 'That must be his wife,' I thought. Suddenly she turned and smiled at me."

Ko-Ko seemed to stop in the middle of his story, and looked at me across the desk with a strange intensity.

"No European woman," he said, "ever smiled at me like that before."

It was his first insight into the possibility that God loves everyone irrespective of the colour of his skin. P'eng-Yu the wild boy had already been won. Unbeknown to Ko-Ko he put his friend's name down for a course of Bible Study.

"So you see," said Ko-Ko, "I received the course through the post and the first thing I began to learn was the meaning and nature of sin. I began to find out just what was wrong with me and why I was so miserable. How can a man ever be happy when out of touch with the One who made him?

"I learned how God's Son died in my place at Calvary.

"I learned how He rose again from the grave.

"I learned that He saves for ever those who put their trust in Him . . .

"Soon I began to go along to that house where you are living now and there we used to sing hymns together and listen to Mr. Pucknell teaching the Bible. Things were changing inside me. I knew it was the only way worth taking. Christ was undoubtedly real and I really wanted His salvation more than anything else.

"One day not long after, I found myself on my own, at home. Father and mother had gone out on a gambling spree. My brother was down at the billiards and my sisters had gone next door. I was all alone in our bedsitting-room. It was a simple place. There was an old wooden bed with a mosquito-net tied over it, and beside the bed was our desk with my school books on it. Somehow I felt very sad and lonely. I looked through the open door. The sun was just setting in deep red over Gaya Island. It was exceedingly beautiful. I watched the people walking slowly along the road outside. Oh, how people forget God, I thought. Oh, how empty is our life without Thee. No peace. No peace. No peace. . . . Suddenly I turned from the doorway. My heart was breaking. Then it was that my eyes caught sight of the little text I had hung so recently on the wall. I looked intently at the clearly printed characters.

" 'God so loved the world that He gave His only begotten Son . . .' it said, and as I read, tears came down my cheeks. Nothing could stop me now. I knew that I was coming back to God. The words of the text ran on, 'that whosoever believeth in Him should not perish but have everlasting life.' "

As I finished reading it, I just bowed my head in my hands, there on the desk. I could think of nothing but the Cross. All I could see was Jesus dying for me.

"As I wept I kept crying out, 'Lord, forgive me! Lord, forgive me!'

"Then as I quietened I simply received Him as my Saviour, and thanked Him with all my heart."

As he finished, Ko-Ko looked at me as if he had some more to say. A brief moment, and then with joy he added, "I *knew* my sins were all forgiven, and I adored Him."

That was the secret then . . .

I rose to go and as I did so dance music came blaring over the partition from the family radio in the next room. Perhaps they would learn the secret soon.

Ko-Ko, after all, was a fisherman!

CHAPTER SIX

JUNGLE RAILCAR

*Between the passages . . . a sharp rock on the one side, and
a sharp rock on the other!*   Samuel

IT was five past one in the morning and I was vaguely conscious
of rain. As each weary moment ticked by I became more and
more conscious that it really was raining; not merely 'cats and
dogs' but the veritable 'water-buffalo' of the North Borneo
monsoon. 'Did we leave the windows open last night or not?'
That was the question. As the torrential heaven-emptying down-
pour lashed the tin roof above my head, sleep began to recede
and I knew only too well the answer was in the affirmative.
'Should I get up?' Visions of water seeping along the lino,
sodden curtains and floods in the sitting-room began to rise in
my mind. Yes, I had better get up. If I stayed in bed I would lie
awake thinking about it. Better to be sleepless and dry than
sleepless and wet. What contortions of senseless reasoning haunt
the man awakened in the early hours. Bravely I fumbled with
the mosquito-net, stood erect for a moment in the darkness and
then began to grope my way from room to room bolting the
wooden shutters in the glassless windows. It was undoubtedly a
blurred and clumsy effort but the children had not wakened and
that was something. I groped my way back, dropped through
the slit in the net, then nearly through the springs, and almost as
quickly into oblivion. . . .

It was five past three. Was it still raining? What had wakened
me this time? A shutter had blown loose, and every few seconds
there was the jarring slam of timber on timber resounding
through the house. It must be stopped. Valiantly I rose again,
located the offender, did the 'necessary', and repeated the
mosquito-net procedure.

What a night of rain! In the tropics rain is not to be despised.

44

Its equatorial proportions are formidable and it has to be reckoned with. Slowly I began to remember something was happening tomorrow, but tomorrow was now today, so it was happening today and rain can affect happenings . . .

That was it! We were going to Tenom. There were ninety miles of narrow railway track winding its way through marshes, jungles and gorges to the interior. How many landslides would be across the track? How many bridges would be washed away? How many trees blocking the lines? I could hardly think how much must have befallen that brief ninety miles of railroad, but the journey to Tenom was almost certainly 'off'. I then began to think of the house. The refrigerator had been emptied, the last bread and butter would be eaten at breakfast, my wife had the children's clothes all packed away. Everything was set to vacate the premises. We had worked to a finish 'burning our bridges' behind us . . . but what if there were no bridges before us? I fell to sleep before the burden of the night became insupportable . . .

Drrrh! I woke with a jolt. The alarm clock was clattering away like a rivetting machine! I knew I could not find the stopper quickly enough so I resigned myself to hearing it out. I looked at the clock. It was five past five. Too early to get up. Too late to sleep again. The night was through. When at last, worn out from trying to rest, I did emerge, the dawn was breaking, the storm clouds had cleared and the sun was shining enthusiastically as if nothing had happened. The fresh atmosphere was all very infectious and within an hour the whole family was not only up but had demolished the last remnants of the said bread and butter; the luggage had been bundled to the door and we were ready for the 'great adventure' of a trip into the interior. Across the way we saw Mrs. Su, our neighbour, the one who used to worship the moon but now was a Christian. We gave her a good wave, then along came one of the red taxis, and we were whisked royally into Jesselton Town Station.

There was no help for it. The clerk simply would insist on calling the stationmaster. It was all because of a little red paint mark on a concrete pillar at the platform entrance. The clerk assured us that he could not act without authority so the stationmaster simply had to be called. Solemnly the stationmaster stood our two small boys against the pillar. There was no hope for Ross. He was three foot eight. That is to say he was eight whole inches over the red mark, but Peter held possibilities. He stood quite innocently whilst the stationmaster measured him. We all waited and then the verdict was pronounced—one and a quarter inches too tall. That one and a quarter inches meant nine dollars to the railway company. All children over three feet tall must pay half fare. The stationmaster looked at the children and then in true oriental benevolence declared, that seeing that there were *two* small boys and that they *were* small, only one would be charged! Peter was 'forgiven'!

We all walked jauntily along the platform to the railcar. This had been our final choice. The real train, known locally as the 'Tenom Train'[1] would leave at half past eight instead of seven o'clock. To do the ninety miles it would need anything between five and twelve hours. In fact the 'Tenom Train' is a real Borneo institution. From cow-catcher to tail-van it is one long bone-shaker. Whether you are a water-buffalo in a goods van or just a buffalo in any other van, you are equally 'buffed' and brought 'low'. Winding its way through the hills it is for all the world like one of those toy serpents made up of separate blocks. You never know whether the particular block you are concerned with is going to go, after all, in the general direction. The 'Tenom Train', whilst catering for both goods and passengers, is really not too good for any passenger. So with the heat and time factor to reckon with, not to mention the possibility of Peter being over three feet tall, we 'embraced' the railcar.

From the start we were delighted with it. Ross and Peter would have taken over the driving had they been asked but as no one asked them they esconced themselves next to us, and close to the driver, where we all commanded an unobstructed view of the track before us. On the tick of the station clock,

[1] Officially, the 'Murut Mail'.

and quite contrary to the usual interpretation of such time-pieces in Borneo, the driver, to our astonishment, took his place at the controls. The railcar was really like a big six-seater car running on railway lines instead of on the roadway. There was an imposing red-painted clutch and a red-painted handbrake just as in a car, but with the rather unnerving aspect of no steering wheel to accompany them. The final complement turned out to be six and a half passengers, Peter being the half! The station-master gave one more flourish of authority and we glided down the track.

The freshness of the morning was magnificent. Slender palms and high grasses stood hushed and still after the wildness of the night. The cool air coursed through the windows giving us the sweetest breath of fresh air we had known six degrees north of the equator. Whrrrr! At each unprotected crossing and foot-path over the line, the railcar's siren let out its unearthly warning. People walking along the track were startled out of their wits and jumped unceremoniously into the mud at the side. At intervals red-and-white flags gave notice of 'men at work' and almost immediately we would pass a group of Dusun and Chinese coolies who might have been bandits had the weapons they were waving been swords and not scythes. Their clothes were little more than a jumble of vests, pants and worn-out pyjamas. They proved quite friendly towards the railcar, thankful, no doubt, for a respite as we passed. Large numbers of men must have been employed over the whole distance. Without them the railway track would disappear beneath the undergrowth in a matter of months.

The last vestiges of the 'Jesselton civilisation' now lay behind us. We gathered speed and passing through extensive belts of sago palms and tangled mangroves we headed out across the swamps into 'unknown' country. Inland, the forested mountains were lifting their heads through wisps of cloud, the closely matted trees with their varied foliage and greenery, giving a sense of woolly texture to the jungle, as it draped the shoulders and long arms of the foothills. Here and there we glimpsed

47

quiet stretches of muddy water holding breathless reflections of the luxuriant branch and leaf above. Gradually the marshes gave way to a wide expanse of rice fields. A delicate carpet of soft watery green, fretted hither and thither with low mud walls terraced gently back to the virgin growth on more distant rising ground. Dotting the tranquillity, grey water-buffalo ambled lazily through the mud, grazing in the fallow acres. After quite a while we came to a station with a long name hard to decipher. Outside the halt was an indifferent row of shops. It seemed a rather drab little place but the bright splash of vermilion bougainvillea that bowed to us on the platform gave a sense of laughter amidst the poverty. Some Dusun women stood sleek and resplendent, girt in their peacock and floral calico, watching us go through. We paused a moment. The stationmaster came out and gave our driver a slip of paper. A brief word passed between them and we were once again on our way.

We had not gone far when we pulled up before a branch line striking away from the main track. The driver opened his door and jumped out. He was one of those people of Borneo who are of undecided nationality. He definitely was not Chinese, certainly not Indian and hardly Dusun or Murut. He had a cheerful bronze face which broke easily into a broad smile. His railway uniform made it even more difficult to determine his identity. Whoever he was, he took his driving very quietly and proceeded at all times quite unperturbed. As we approached a point, I saw it was guarded by a huge handle. Halting the vehicle, our driver pulled out a key from his pocket. Whatever was he going to do? He very soon shewed us. Proceeding to the handle he applied his key to a large padlock. Once this was removed he pulled the handle back and the point ground rustily into position. Back he jumped into the cabin, drove our vehicle a few yards forward, then dismounting, readjusted the point, locked it again and leaped back into his seat. Such is life on the railway in North Borneo! Once again we proceeded and began to scan the lovely countryside. Blue smoke was lifting through the nipa palm leaf roofs of the native huts. I caught the scarlet splash of a tulip tree, and the red sheaths of numerous palms standing up like witches' brooms ready for take-off. On open stretches the ground was possessed by a broad-leaved shrub with large yellow flowers. Then came the rubber plantations. There is a sense of sadness as you view the slender young rubber trees and know that they will grow to gnarled old giants slashed and scarred all down the stem. Between the rubber trees, pineapples had been planted, but soon the rubber trees yielded to open country and we noticed many kingfishers in iridescent turquoise fleeting from the telegraph wires towards the jungle. Stacks of wood carefully cut and neatly piled, lay at the side of the track ready for collection. A rise in the ground ahead brought us rather unexpectedly to a tunnel. Sitting as we were, with the driver, it was rather like driving a tube train in Britain. Ross and Peter were immediately on the alert. We plunged into the semi-darkness and away in the distance we could see the little round hole leading out into the light. As we approached it, a large number of swallows were criss-crossing at high speed in front of the train. You could see their little forms darting frantically to and fro against the light.

We passed through Papar and eventually pulled into Beaufort. The Beaufort of today is comprised mostly of large blocks of shops and flats raised well off the ground, for the river Padas sometimes causes serious flooding in the town. During the Japanese occupation, Beaufort was the military capital of North Borneo. This was the first major town to be captured by the Japanese forces, entering through Weston, some distance to the south. It continued as their headquarters until June 1945. Then the 9th Australian Division commanded by General Wooten landed at Labuan, overcame opposition, and launched an attack on the Japanese in Beaufort. The town was liberated and the entire Japanese administration foundered almost immediately. As we looked at Beaufort that day, all was peaceful. Every scar of war had been removed. A good percentage of the population would not even remember a Japanese. So war passes and only the older hearts carry their sorrows to the grave.

After a brief break all the ticket-holders were aboard again for the passage of the gorges. As we left Beaufort the country changed and the narrow-gauge track clung perilously to the hill-sides as we began to follow the tortuous defile of the Padas river up through the mountains to Tenom. We had our first glimpse of the river soon after leaving the town. At first it flowed placidly, a broad, slow, copper-coloured swirl of water, figured occasionally by eddies, and moving quietly down to the sea. But as the valley narrowed the waters flowed more swiftly. On some stretches the bamboo grew in huge feathery umbrellas close to the edge but jungle growth thickened and our views became more obscured. Occasionally, however, we could look up long reaches of the river which afforded us vistas of great beauty. The mountainsides now became precipitous and clad with impenetrable rain-forests. Huge trees with long smooth trunks, and no branches for about the first fifty feet, towered majestically above the lower vegetation. A fantastic entangle-ment of drooping tendrils, intertwined with a galloping growth of forest. Down through the riot of greenery the river now frothed and foamed. The little railcar skipped over the narrow bridges and through the gulleys. Bevies of black butterflies flitted about the rocks that hemmed us in. Occasional wild bananas leaned out to meet us. It was well we did not try to snatch them for the leaves and branches of the jungle trees are often full of leeches. Narrower and narrower the valley became. The roar of the waters shouted up to us from below. Over the jumbled boulders the maelstrom plunged like a hoard of wild horses in a furious helter-skelter down the chasm. In the few quieter stretches odd native huts nestled silently along the muddy and sandy shore and I found my mind going away to Palm Beach in the heart of Equador. In the vast back-waters of the Amazon it was just the same kind of country, the same kind of heat and the same jungle. I thought of Jim Elliot and his friends falling under a shower of spears in that lonely place, that the Aucas might hear about Jesus. What did he say? "He is no fool who gives what he cannot keep to gain what he cannot lose." It was good to be in Borneo for Christ's sake. High up over the trees the sun and cloud reflected the spiritual struggle in the skies. I looked at the expanse of blue. Is there anything greater than total commitment to the Lord of all? Every life and every journey has its destiny and destination. At the next station a couple of rough looking characters came in at the back of us, fondling shot-guns. "What do you shoot?" I asked. "Wild pig," one of them grunted, and about thirty minutes later we were rattling down the straight into Tenom Town.

CHAPTER SEVEN

CROCODILE TOWN

Teeth as swords . . .
Jaw-teeth as knives.   Proverbs

TENOM has lived for years waiting to be devoured. The voracious jaws of the Padas gorge have but to protrude the river's foaming tongue into the wide valley and the busy country town would lie silent for ever. In a certain year now fast merging into more distant history someone proposed damming the gorge. It was at once an appealing and appalling suggestion which gained currency in general conversation, if not at once in government circles. It would ensure a splendid water supply for people other than the Tenomites. Hydro-electric schemes could supply electricity to a wide area exclusive of the immediate valley. As the suggestion moved towards a decision it seemed that the death sentence was virtually passed on Tenom. Land prices fell to near zero. A pall of stagnation and aroma of death crept through the community. Many left. Few came. After a long while someone else made another suggestion. The plan for a giant reservoir should be delayed. The death sentence was thus suspended although not commuted. Land prices lifted just a dollar or two. A faint whiff of fresh air stirred through the becalmed economy. Tenom after all might live, then why not live in Tenom? The damage, however, was done. To this day this lovely little township nestling in the hills of old Murut country, and commanding the produce of a fine fertile plain is still like an unwanted baby.

As our tiny railcar crawled slowly from the opening jaws of this Padas gorge there was an immediate sense of tranquillity, amounting almost to relief. The flanges of the wheels no longer ground and grated on the track. Effortlessly we glided forward. We had reached a broad plateau which after the tortuous climb gave one the impression of being at a great elevation although we were probably no more than six hundred feet up. We caught our first glimpse of a motor road since leaving the coastal strip. It rose steeply out of the river where a primitive ferry plied to and fro loaded with jeeps and lorries.

At last we reached the station. Our eyes were strained to see who would be there to meet us. In the brilliant sunshine we dropped out of the railcar on to the platform, like mutilated sardines being disgorged from a partly opened tin. There was George, a fearless Scot with a heart of gold and a fist of iron, with his wife Phyllis and their quiver of youngsters who will always speak Chinese better than Gaelic. With them stood David and Betty Smith. The last time I saw them was on their wedding day in a scene of pressed suits and butterfly orchids at the Jesselton Hotel. They had now been married just five months and it was good to meet them in the simple surroundings of the Borneo interior getting on with their language study. Beyond the station lay the few streets of shops, and above, the jungle-covered hills rose into a misty blue sky. Once the luggage had been separated from the children and the available masculine hands filled with the heavier cases, we trooped like a colony of settlers out from the little railway station towards the big green which dominates the centre of Tenom. For months in Jesselton we had been working at high pressure. My wife had been helping in some voluntary occupational therapy in the T.B. Hospital and I myself had been preaching and teaching almost continuously. As we arrived now in this country town, the tension seemed suddenly to relax and we really began to feel on holiday.

After refreshing ourselves at the Rest House we made our first sortie into the town. The most distinctive feature is the splendid open space that brightens the whole neighbourhood. Here the schools play off their basket-ball and football matches, native and Chinese festivities take place, and also captive crocodiles from the river are put on display. The way Tenom deals with its crocodiles is quite bizarre. George told me of an interesting case. One day a man suddenly disappeared whilst swimming in the river and the next day his body was found with one arm bitten off near the shoulder. This was without doubt the work of a crocodile. This 'crime' meant that a crocodile had broken the ancient pact, which according to local tradition was concluded in past ages between crocodiles and mankind. It is only when a crocodile kills someone that the people of Tenom will kill a crocodile. Otherwise they, that is the crocodiles, are allowed to breed and molest unhindered. In these extreme and dastardly circumstances the local people had no other recourse but to employ a professional crocodile hunter to deal with the enemy. Whilst this procedure is enshrouded with superstition, the actual catching of the crocodile is undoubtedly a remarkable feat and carried out by an unexplained and mysterious process. When the hunter arrives, he is led to the scene of the attack on the unfortunate victim. Waiting until nightfall the hunter pushes off into the river in a small boat. It is completely dark and he is alone. In some peculiar way he then 'calls' the crocodile. This is the secret technique passed on, no doubt, from father to son. Whatever it is that the hunter does, he is successful in obtaining a comparatively quick surfacing of a crocodile, which then comes quite peacefully to his canoe. The hunter at once harpoons it in a vulnerable spot with a barbed spear mounted on a long bamboo pole. Once struck, the crocodile lunges back and the harpoon head comes off leaving a length of rope running in the water. At this juncture the hunter jumps into the river (a most hazardous undertaking), grasps the rope, reaches out for the shore and the crocodile is hauled in. They are tremendous creatures and un-controllable in their own element but these hunters by methods known only to themselves, seem to have a strange control over them. Single-handed the crocodile is defeated. The beast is then trussed and carried alive the next morning to the big open green in the centre of Tenom Town. The peculiar thing now is, that the hunter refuses to kill the crocodile. He will catch it but not kill it. This probably has something to do with the pact. The actual killing of the crocodile is carried out in a semi-official manner by pole axe. The beast is then dissected to find out whether any of the victim's belongings, for example a ring or money, are in its stomach so that full identification can be made of the culprit. The post-mortem having been made, the skin goes to the hunter and the meat to the people who hired him. The Government also issue a reward determined by the neck measurement of the hapless creature. As we reached the far side of the green we entered on a road that led us towards George Hanlon's home. The transport in the town is almost exclusively Land-Rover jeeps and Toyotas.[1] These are the buses, lorries and taxis of the entire district and it is possible to travel up on rough roads to Keningau, and finally to Tambunan, where the mountains rise to eight thousand feet.

Amongst a riot of vegetation and garden flowers lay a wooden house with a corrugated iron roof. It was raised several feet above the earth, being supported by high concrete piles. With the help of a few carpenters George had built it himself. I looked at it, amazed at such an effort in the tropical heat of Borneo. "I prefabricated it," he said easily, "and the first day we began to build, we put it up to the eaves." The townsfolk were astounded and wondered who this strong man was that had come to town. Apparently when George had first come, people were not very willing to rent premises, refusing to re-accommodate their idols for the sake of Christian missionaries, thus eventually the herculean task was attempted. Once up, however, the trouble began. Unconsciously George's house had been built facing the opposite way from everybody else's. The direction he chose was, naturally enough, with the front of the house facing the best scenery. Soon the neighbours became perturbed, saying that the geomancy of the area had not been investigated. "Would George please turn his house round the other way." The spirits of the hills would be offended and in the interest of the local people he should do something about it. George could only give an emphatic Scots "No!" It was more than he could ever undertake to do. Shortly afterwards the local

[1] A Japanese vehicle like a jeep.

authorities opened a new road at the foot of the hills and George's house was the only one with a frontage on it. Gradually the people began to change their mind. The sound sense of the Christian missionary at last prevailed.

As we clambered up the steps and entered into the cooler precincts of the home we began to see something of the heroism and hard work that characterises missionary families slogging it out in the uttermost parts. Simple, fresh, clean and in the realest sense holy. That is to say, a place where children are reared thriftily but joyfully, where pleasures are simple but appreciated, where over all there is the sense that this place exists for the glory of the living God and the extension of His Kingdom. There was the atmosphere of sacrifice but not of severity, of very real standards, yet merged with kindliness and good humour. I had known George in his early days in China when his head was as red as a flame and every iota of truth was worth dying for. His hair was browner now. His resolute character had been expressed in deeds, and he did not need so much to say what he believed. He had acted in the last fifteen years and his work could speak. It is interesting to note that once our Lord Jesus Christ had completed His work at the Cross he never spoke to the world at large again. He did not need to. It is because youth has not yet achieved that it is so vociferous.

"Do you recall that day we climbed the mountain in Kiangsi in China," he said, "and how we raced up to the summit in the blazing heat, just about killing ourselves?"

"Only our pride carried us there," I said; "not one of us would give in!" Since then we had found other mountains to climb and we had needed something more than pride to get us there. Years in the Tibetan border and Communist prisons in my case, and years in the Borneo outback in his had left their mark on both of us and it was so good to meet again and rejoice together in the patient God who perseveres with us even when we fail.

A large part of the home was given over to a meeting room where several times a week Christians in Tenom would congregate, meeting very simply in Jesus' Name, to read His Word and to worship Him. When God scans the earth it may well be that little groups like this command His attention whilst the great cathedrals are left to the sightseer and the tourist. "Our rejoicing is this," says Paul, "the testimony of our conscience, that in simplicity and godly sincerity not with fleshly wisdom we have had our conversation in the world."

As we talked, the children raced round the garden, that used to be the jungle but was now a broad lawn lined with yellow cosmos. European children are a source of astonishment to the rural Chinese and natives. Firstly they are so big and often 'fat'. To say a baby is 'fat' is the last thing you would say in Tenom. The people maintain that such 'praise' will be heard by eavesdropping demons who will take note of the child and cause it to waste away under their malignant and baneful spells. Then, too, white babies are said to be operated on at birth and their appendix immediately removed. As for their heads these are considered quite unfashionable. The Chinese babies have elegant flat heads whilst European babies are just allowed to 'bulge'. Chinese mothers often lay their babies on their backs between two pillows. In this way they are prevented from turning over and their 'flat heads' are assured. Regarding the hazards the children face from the tropical insect world, we found we were not alone in our concern. George told us how one day he killed a large bee. Forty minutes later his little daughter picked it up and put it in her mouth. She received a sting on her lip, and her whole face on one side was swollen for three days. It was a merciful escape as some of the large bees, huge black creatures, can give a fatal sting, especially to children. On the centipede question we related how Ross had picked up a piece of corrugated iron at Tanjong Aru and found himself face to face with a centipede about five inches long and as thick as a man's finger. At this George gaily produced a whole bottle full of these creatures. When he caught one he put it in spirit and squeezed out the poison. The resulting liquid, after a while, proved an antidote for anyone stung by these vicious insects. "Primitive homeopathy!" he triumphantly exclaimed. These centipedes can also sting a child to death. Snakes, of course, there are too, but not so many as might be imagined and they usually will not attack unless disturbed.

Just a stone's throw from the house stood the Chinese temple. It was a filthy looking hovel of a place reminiscent to me of the stench and wretchedness that characterises the old pagodas in China. Here on occasions it was possible to see a demon-possessed woman dancing in the forecourt going through contortions, screaming hideously, or on the other hand, the red flow of blood from the slaughter of pigs for sacrifice. It is the 'business' of the temple folk to deal with demon-disturbance throughout the neighbourhood. The common practice is to burn joss sticks before the affected house. This is followed by the scattering of rice towards the east during the hours of darkness, accompanied by the burning of paper money. Such is the formula for pacifying a hungry demon. If a stray dog comes to eat the rice, then more than likely, the dog is viewed as the personification of the demon! Such a futile admixture of the sinister and the ridiculous makes up the dark, superstitious and enslaving background of the people of Tenom. It is not in vain that God sends His emissaries to the far frontiers of humanity. There is only one Name that saves.

CHAPTER EIGHT

HOBGOBLIN OR FOUL FIEND?

Terrors . . . on every side!   Bildad

SHUT your eyes in Borneo and think of England. Where are the demons?

Hedge-rows in Devon, tube trains in London, a postman at the door, daffodils in the park, strawberries in June, bonfires in November. Motorways, collars and ties, newspaper boys and fish and chip shops. Old people going to church in their best clothes, teddy boys and their rock 'n roll. This is the panorama of England, the dull and the bright of it unfolding willy-nilly in the mind of the exile. Where would the road of thought and memory run out at last? Probably to a fireside on a winter's evening, or, maybe, to an old mother's lips. When, however, the reverie of daydream and the spell of fantasy are broken, the question still remains, "Are there demons no more in England?" Actually there are, but of course they keep them in little boxes carefully indexed under inscrutable psychological names. In Borneo they also have names for them. No one understands them there either but the superstitious native of the East is often more in touch with reality than the supercilious intelligentsia of the West.

The ambassador of Christ standing at the ends of the earth in this twentieth century finds himself confronted with a modern high school at one end of the street and an incense-filled heathen temple at the other. The two institutions speak a different 'language' but too often serve a common master. Atheism and polytheism will, however, both prove ultimately disastrous. What remains is the reality of a personal devil operating through pseudo-intellectualism on the student and through superstition on the peasant. The man sent of God must stand in each case against the perverted imagination of the human heart and bring people face to face with Christ, who is not only the All Wise God but the One who contended with a real devil, in really human circumstances. Denial of the devil is equally foolish as active submission to him. The missionary stands to bring every thought into captivity to Christ. The parroting-student of the high school and gibbering-slave of the temple can only know their liberation in personal surrender to the Most High. The recognition of and obedience to the purpose of Him who made them is the only way to freedom. Their shackles will only be lost in choosing to obey. The missionary goes then not merely to persuade, but to command repentance and obedience to the Name of God revealed in Jesus Christ.

In this task the work of Satan ceases to be an item of discussion. The Christian worker must get on with the fighting. From the back parts of Borneo and more especially from the Chinese settlers comes the following selection of incidents which when placed together gives at least some idea of the pathetic darkness of these distant places and the great need for the salvation that only Christ can bring.

"Recently," said a missionary, "I visited the home of a Chinese who was a spirit-medium. He was a friendly-looking old fellow of about fifty-five or so. As I stepped into his home I was almost immediately aware of an altar shelf on the other side of the room, which was dominated by five female porcelain figures, each about eight inches high. Before the idols were spread the usual offerings of wine, fruit and other food. I looked at the idols and began to ask the old man about them.

" 'Oh,' he said, 'the spirits visit me very often, in fact you could say, just about every other night once darkness is down. Sometimes,' he went on, his eyes becoming wild and staring, 'high personages amongst the "gods" commune with me and I have visions of shining dragons and horses.' I surveyed him half-sceptically but he was speaking in obvious sincerity and vowed that he was telling me the truth.

" 'These spirits,' he continued, 'give me information about all the deaths and illnesses for miles around. For example,' he said, 'when my younger brother, working on one of the rubber estates near here, died, the spirits let me know. I also get information about the activities going on in the temple in town . . .'

"Christ is utterly supreme over all these powers," I said and handed him a Gospel to read, "Only He can save from the powers of darkness."

" 'Christians,' he grunted, 'I'll tell you something about Christians. Their "characters", that is the Chinese Characters by which people are identified to their mediums, are like those of foreigners and not like other Chinese.' What did he mean? Of course he was speaking as a medium. After a while I left the old man and walked out into the sunshine. Perhaps the day would come when he would seek the sunshine too."

Dealing with mediums and their alleged powers of insight to local affairs, there was the rather astute comment of the female medium installed during a revival of superstition and idolatry at the Keningau temple. For quite a while people flocked every week-end to the temple to consult her on all sorts of matters. Amongst these, there was a man who had especially travelled from Jesselton to test her ability. He himself was also a medium but doubted the claims of this woman. He was, it is said, completely unknown to her and she found it necessary to have recourse to her familiar spirit. The reply came much to his chagrin, "People of the same trade should not compete with one another!" This greatly enhanced her reputation amongst her followers.

Satanic delusions, however, are not confined to the practising mediums, for the ordinary folk are full of accounts of what they themselves have seen of the supernatural. Such accounts even appear in the daily papers and are given great credence. Like the 'flying saucers' of the West we are left wondering, can sheer hallucination account for all that sincere and honest people have professed to see? In March 1960 a Chinese newspaper published the following account.

"Most people in Keningau are able to tell you of some news which has the appearance of a spiritual mystery . . . When this

61

strange affair unexpectedly took place, there were many eye-witnesses. With hands doing more than mouths (that is with many gesticulations) all told the same story and the report now given would appear to be real news. I (the reporter) have personally interviewed all concerned and now present the general picture.

"In the interior, on the banks of the Pinpany River, the wife and family of a motor driver at 3 p.m. on the third of March were sitting in the doorway of their home resting. Suddenly in the sky above their roof they saw what appeared to be a man clothed in silvery white garments. He stood stationary in space. The weather was clear and visibility good so that this 'heavenly man' was clearly seen. Beneath his feet was a cloud and eventually he ascended slowly and gracefully into the blue. When the woman and her children saw this strange sight they called a neighbouring family to make sure they were not mistaken." The report was fully accepted and believed by the local people.

A similar incident was recounted by a missionary friend who went to great lengths to verify the story. "The mother of two boys in a nearby school went with her daughter to visit their new home. This was situated across a river. As they made their way in the fading light they saw something shining brightly, and gradually descending the mountainside. They were both very frightened. As the object came closer they could see it was an angel (that is how they described it). It was white and shining, had wings and was later followed by a number of childlike figures all flying and glowing. The mother and her daughter managed to retreat into the house but the larger figure followed. The mother then tried to restrain it but it eluded her and disappeared away up the hill. The next night her two boys went to investigate and they swore that they saw a bright light shining away in the jungle. Cross questioning could not shake them from their story." As one hears of such accounts so strangely linked with Biblical descriptions, the words 'No marvel . . . Satan himself is transformed into an angel of light' come readily to mind.

One of the questions I have been asked since living in Borneo is, "Do spirits harm human beings?" My answer was the incident in Luke's Gospel, "And lo a spirit taketh him and he suddenly crieth out; and it teareth him that he foameth again, and, bruising him, hardly departed from him." Mark records it like this, "... and wheresoever he taketh him, he teareth him; and he foameth, and gnasheth with his teeth and pineth away ... he fell on the ground and wallowed foaming."

A Mr. Wong moved into a new house in Tenom which he had managed to buy very cheaply. He was very distressed though, because at night the children became terrified crying out that 'something' was trying to strangle them. It so happened that two children had died in that house before he bought it. He believed that the spirits of the dead children were returning to trouble them as the new residents. This is supposed to be a common occurrence and no amount of talking will dissuade people from this interpretation of such circumstances. The Bible gives no evidence that the spirits of deceased persons return. In fact the story of the rich man and Lazarus show that this is impossible, but the impersonation of the departed is no doubt undertaken by fallen spirit beings seeking a body for expression. That such evil spirits do seek such embodiment even in the animal world is seen in the story of the healing of the demon-possessed man in Gadara, where Christ permits the evil spirits to enter the herd of swine. The case quoted from Mark and Luke refers to a child and it is appalling to think that the evil one is able to molest young children in these ways. The 'explaining away' of particular incidents can never abolish the evidence of all the incidents on record, of an active malignant molesting spiritual power behind the evils of the world.

Another case that came to my knowledge was of a young woman, and was even more striking. It happened about ninety miles from Jesselton. She had just been married and all seemed well. Suddenly she disappeared and the local people organised a great search for her. The extraordinary thing was, that no trace of her could be found, yet a week later she was found still alive in a rubber plantation. She was filthy-dirty and thoroughly dishevelled. She had been eating handfuls of earth and seemed to be out of her mind. Once she was taken home she gradually began to recover until she was able to tell her story. She said that she had been attacked by a demon, who wanted her for his wife. She had found it impossible to resist the fiend and he had driven her away. She seemed to be able to relate little else. The stories of people being led away by demons are numerous in Borneo.

Another woman, a Mrs. Chung, was very sad because she had borne no children. As a last resort she went to the heathen temple in Tenom where she submitted to certain rites in order to obtain fertility and surprisingly enough, within a period of just a few years, she gave birth to four children. In the process, however, she yielded to a demon possession, giving herself over to Satan. Twice she tried to cut her own throat and her screams were enough to make the blood run cold.

The Western mind may quibble at such accounts. Science may endeavour to explain a malady even where it is powerless to heal but Jesus knew what He was doing when confronted with such cases. We read, "He rebuked the foul spirit, saying I charge thee . . . come out of him and enter no more into him." The Name of Jesus is still effective today for this work and at that Name the entire fallen spirit world trembles and awaits its doom.

A Mr. Wen told how not long after his conversion he and his wife were wakened by the noise of 'his sister's voice' crying to them. It was very unnerving for his sister had been dead several years. "Give up Christ!" she screamed. "Give up Christ! Curses on you for abandoning your old beliefs." This was not just a moment's imagination on waking, but continued through the night in a most terrifying manner. Such is the devil's hostility to Jesus' Name.

Out of such a world of spirits, real and imaginary as the different cases may be, God is bringing men, women and children to the calm security of His mighty Hand. As they trust the Lord Jesus His unchanging Word declares, "They shall never perish . . . none shall pluck them from my hand . . . I and my Father are one."

One bright Sunday morning I stood in several feet of water with a young man. But a short while before, following a meeting for the preaching of the Gospel, he had lingered behind and we had talked of spiritual things for about an hour. After a thorough consideration of his problems in the light of the Bible, he had knelt on the floorboards and yielded himself whole-heartedly to Christ. He was from an idolatrous home where even the food was offered to the images before eating. Now he was finished with it all. I grasped his clothes firmly at his back and he clasped my hand. "Do you believe in the Lord Jesus Christ as your own personal Saviour and Lord?" I asked him. About us were gathered a crowd of Chinese, Indians and Europeans. "I do," he said and I felt his grip tighten. It was meaning everything to him. "Then on your personal confession and at your own request, I baptise you in the Name of the Father, and of the Son, and of the Holy Ghost." He passed beneath the waters. "Old things were passed away." He emerged. "All things had become new."

Christ Jesus has made His victory ours. "The gates of hell shall not prevail," not even in Borneo.

CHAPTER NINE

IN OLD BLOW-PIPE COUNTRY

A book of remembrance was written before Him for them that
feared the Lord, and thought upon His Name.   Malachi

FROM the bowl of the lush green hills a rough gravel track runs
out to the river. Beyond, through the broken jungle and the
encroaching plantations live the Chinese settlers and the Murut
natives. The virgin growth is receding before the coffee and
rubber estates and natives are coming down from the hills,
abandoning their predatory livelihood and being integrated into
the more peaceful pursuits of agriculture inspired by Chinese
capital and industry. It is a great stretch of country, still ragged
with charred hulks of trees and half-cleared land. Through
undulating folds and shallow valleys it looks like some rough
patchwork quilt sown intermittently with maize, coffee and
rubber. Here and there the dog-eared kapok tree fluffs its dangling pods to the breeze or the stark white trunk of a 'graveyard
giant' stretches its mighty boughs a hundred feet above the road.

The day we hired the jeep dawned fine and dry, and equipped
with sandwiches and water-bottles we clambered into it, set for a
day in the outback country. We raced a bit for the ferry, as the
men operating it break off at certain times. At last a gap in the
trees brought us to the water's edge. Downstream there lay a
fine vista of the narrowing gorges and straight ahead on the
bosom of the water was the primitive ferry straining at the long
hawser spanning the river. The little outboard motor attached
to the side of the long float, chugged patiently through the
muddy stream taking a total load of only two vehicles each
time. We had some while to wait but the pleasantness of the
spot compensated for the delay. It was here that George Hanlon
met a patriarchal old man one day crossing the ferry. He was
seventy-eight and had a special air of venerability with unusually

white hair and flowing beard. "I used to be a medium," he said, "and had visions of dragons and spirits in the sky. I even spoke with demons in those days—but one day as I was crossing the ferry there came to me all unexpectedly, the vision of a man. I am sure it was the Lord Jesus. He told me to turn from my evil practices and cleave to the Lord. I immediately obeyed Him. That is how I became a Christian." As George spoke of the reality of heaven and the welcome that awaits the redeemed, the eyes of the old man shone and a joy filled his face. "Last of all," says Paul, "He was seen of me." Whether it be on the banks of the Jordan, the Thames or the Padas, each saint knows that personal encounter with the Lord which changes him for ever.

Once on the ferry with the clay-coloured waters hurrying menacingly beneath us, we looked for crocodiles. A big twenty-five footer had been circling some days earlier but today there was no break in the sullen surface of the water. We safely reached the farther bank, boarded the jeep again and headed out along the track, leaving a trail of billowing dust and sand behind us. On our right we soon came to a huge rubber estate. It had just changed hands for five million dollars. At the roadside was a line of 'pedigree' rubber trees. These were all registered with the Government. Any such trees found growing elsewhere in the colony would indicate a theft of these particular seeds. In this way the owners are protected. We lumbered into Sapong. The houses were white-washed wooden structures. The bullet holes from the war still scarred the timber. We paused for a short while and I went into the village shop to greet an old Chinese friend. He was a Christian from the church in Tanjong Aru. He had been cruelly exploited in Jesselton and against his wishes forced to sell idolatrous paraphernalia to the public. At last he had left, getting an opening in Sapong village. He greeted me with Christian gladness and it was good to see him radiant for God in this distant place. He was beginning to talk to the village children about the Lord Jesus. So God fulfils His Word, 'And they shall hear to whom no tidings of Him came.'

As we penetrated farther, streams began to cross the road. There had been little rain and we were able to ford them without difficulty, although George in flooded conditions had his motor bicycle swept from under him and carried away downstream. It took six Muruts to drag it up the bank. Ten miles out and we saw a cleared site. Missionaries together with the local people had sweated in the broiling sun to prepare the ground for the building of a meeting place where believers might regularly gather and services be held. It may have taken centuries, but nevertheless the conquest of Calvary begins to reach to the last dark boundaries of the earth.

At Mile Fifteen we turned in suddenly off the road, to be welcomed fervently by the little group of Christians, who with others hope soon to have their own chapel. Meanwhile they met in the simple home of one of their number. On either side of us stretched fields of maize already seven feet high. An immense tree arched above, and away in the distance, clouds were gathering over the skyline of the hills. We walked across the sunbaked mud of the courtyard and entered through the doorway. Rough planks, corrugated iron, pasteboard and a concrete floor put together as best they knew, made up the primitive house. Our host was a tall, thin Chinese between forty and fifty. He welcomed us warmly, standing there in his rough un-ironed shirt, calico trousers and unlaced sandshoes. His wife, a tiny little woman, was there also, in a white blouse with long sleeves and a figured length of orange-coloured cloth swathed around her. We were standing in the one main room. Its only adornment was five long mirrors inscribed with red Chinese characters. A few prized bits of floral wallpaper are pinned across the bare floorboards. Two antiquated pendulum clocks cling to the pasteboard walls. The friends beckon us to sit down. It is not every day that they have a visit by Christians from abroad. On the table, covered with a white plastic cloth overprinted with brown and yellow circles, innumerable hard-boiled eggs are now served, together with glasses of sweet, fresh coffee. This is their staple beverage. After we have refreshed ourselves, some wicker chairs and benches are pulled into position and a mixed group of Chinese settlers gather to hear the preaching of the Word of God. George stood up and began to speak fluently in the Hakka dialect. Knowing only Mandarin, I found it difficult to follow and my eyes wandered round the bare room. Faded paper chains hung from the roof. They had been at one time, I guess, red, green and yellow. A Tilley lamp also hung from a beam, the only sure illumination in these more undeveloped parts. Soiled topees and some rags hung from nails. A collection of bottles stood on a ledge. Through a doorway I could see a kind of outhouse and an old Thermos flask, an enamel mug and a baby's bottle on a table. In the meeting some of the older Chinese men were now standing up to pray. So simple an approach to the Almighty from this little shack in the Borneo interior, but they could come to Him in Jesus' Name. Had not the Master said so? After a little while, another Chinese brother stood and read a portion of Scripture. To do so, however, he slipped round the corner into a recess. I found out afterwards that he felt self-conscious. He was wearing spectacles for the first time! As George explained the passage I could tell he was speaking of the Lord washing the disciples' feet. I looked up at the little calendar pinned on the wall. The Chinese character said simply *K'an wo ti shou*—"Behold my hands!" Yes, hands that took a towel. Hands that knew the harsh thrust of a jagged nail. Hands that took up the fisherfolk of Galilee and made them immortal for God. The same hands fashioning anew the Chinese settlers of Borneo. This is His work. In the quietness a puppy came bowling in and sat scratching himself. A chicken stalked around between our feet and, as the preaching continued, a Murut woman came in to clear the glasses away, but nobody seemed to notice. Above us the wind was blowing through the open boards. Soon the meeting quietly closed. They had met with Jesus again today. Outside it was beginning to thunder and there was the smell of rain over the jungle. We must be on our way but first a few photos and then farewell. Where shall we meet again? If not in the shacks of Borneo—then in His mansions in the skies. Such are the bonds forged in the blood of Christ, reaching out across the seas, and embracing the nations in the love of God.

The jeep rattled down over the dirt track, lurched up through the coffee fields until we halted at a little village. The rain had now caught up with us and a party of dishevelled Murut women were sheltering in a shop. Outside was a dapper little fellow— a real pigmy of the forest people. He had a blow-pipe—a hollow pole some seven or eight feet long, and poisoned darts at the ready. He showed them to us and then shot a dart at a papaya tree some distance away. Straight to its mark it went. Both he and ourselves grinned with satisfaction. It was not so long ago that those darts would have sunk into our flesh if we had dared to venture through that area—but the Gospel is winning in the ancient blow-pipe country and not only the Chinese settlers, but the Muruts also, are turning to Christ.

CHAPTER TEN

WHERE THE ORCHID BLOOMS

Break forth into singing, O forest, and every tree therein.
Isaiah

IT was *Tamu* time in Tenom. That is the equivalent of saying it was Bank Holiday Monday on Hampstead Heath or Fair Saturday in Glasgow. For many days the momentum of preparation had been gathering and now at long last little stalls of bamboo and *atap*[1] were springing up all around the *padang*.[2] An imposing Chinese gateway, shiny with bright red paint, lifted its proud head high above the fresh green grass. For a brief day or two it would be as the 'Gate of Heavenly Peace' to this little country town. Groups of Muruts and Dusuns were arriving now, filtering in from their homes in the hills. Shopkeepers, food vendors, hawkers and costermongers, 'fun of the fair' folk and a host of others were feverishly fixing their stands. Extra 'Tenom Trains', their carriages crammed with visitors, were beginning to arrive. Was there ever a day like the day of the *Tamu*? All Borneo seemed to have congregated. The quiet, dusty roads, unused to many feet, had now suddenly leapt into activity. Streams of men and women attired in all manner of costumes and speaking a babel of tongues, thronged jauntily through the town.

Singing, talking, laughing, eating, buying, selling, dancing and prancing, they jostled one another in high spirits and with a very real measure of goodwill. There was not a dull moment. Plenty of company, plenty of noise, plenty to see, something for everybody. There were magnified mosquitoes on the anti-malaria stall and beauty queens on the native dance floor. There were cold, wet fish from Borneo's waters and live, furry animals from Borneo's steamy forests. There were gigantic examples of

[1] Malay—*Atap:* thatching.　　　　　　　　[2] *Padang:* village green.

71

equatorial fruits, and knick-knacks, what-nots, 'rags, bottles and bones', at the secondhand stalls. There were native products from the jungle and modern electrical equipment from Jesselton. It was a veritable melting pot of races, cultures, crafts and customs. The meeting point of two extremities of history and the evidence that whoever we are, we all love a bit of excitement.

From a social standpoint, the *Tamus* render quite a service to the community, as not only do they quicken commerce in the interior, but they tend to draw out from the hills, secluded groups of Dusun and Murut tribesmen, to make a first contact with the outside world. The organising authorities, who work hard for the *Tamus* behind the scenes, have been rewarded with no small success in this regard!

Like all these events, however, there is a 'flash in the pan' touch about it. In a little while everyone would return to the jungle and the hard toil of the plantations would be resumed. All would go back to their villages and Tenom would sleep once more. In one sense much would have changed hands, but when all had been said and done, nothing would have changed very much. Behind the glitter and glamour of the moment there was still the poverty and toil of the years. It reminded me of my boyhood, when I went to the fair and won a goldfish. It seemed so great a win, and I 'escorted' my little goldfish back to my home with pride and care. It was so golden but so short-lived. Only three weeks passed and I had to bury it, using an empty soap carton for a coffin. Later on, to my mother's disapproval, I dug it up, only to find it reduced to dust and bones. For many at this Borneo fair it would terminate just like that. It would be the Cinderella story without the happy ending. There was pathos after all in the few days' pageantry.

On the first night of the *Tamu* I stepped out of the house and walked on to the roadway. Where I stood was far from the hurly-burly of the town and the very quietness of the evening brought a benison to the soul. How good it was just to be alive and with eyes to see. I looked upward in the brief and fading twilight. There was a gentleness in the heavens above. The pale

72

face of the moon was glistening wistfully through the delicate veil of a mackerel sky and the darkening hills and forests lay in sombre stillness waiting for the night. Reluctantly I turned, and began to walk towards the clamorous streets. Distant sounds gradually increased until I moved into the full orbit of a bedlam of voices and music. People, people, people, infinitely more enthralling than all the exhibits put together. On every side there were varied colours and conditions of men. I watched a Murut. Where did he come from, this little man of the jungle? His head-dress was magnificent with its long, white plumes and his immaculate coiffure, finished with a dagger stuck through a ball of his thick, black hair. He was girt fiercely at the waist and buttocks with a red band of native cloth, and his small brown body lit up strangely under the freshly installed lighting of the Tenom streets. For all the world it was like a stage, the enacting of some charade or burlesque under the glare of footlights. To look at him, 'heads' might have been had for the hunting just down by the river, but all that was a forgotten story now. Nearby were a group of Dusun women, also quite small of stature but stately in their walk, tightly swathed in figured calico and attractively draped about the shoulders with their colourful coatees. I watched the Chinese once again, surely the most ubiquitous of all the peoples of the East. How indomitable in suffering, how unflagging in labour, how undismayed in poverty! Though I had lived and suffered with them perhaps more than most men, yet in many ways they remain as inscrutable as ever. Voices, voices, voices. What a confusion of reverberations. The blare of jazz from the crude picture-house nearby, the hooting of the jeeps, the screeching of the juke-boxes, the under-hum of the insects, the razzle-dazzle of the whole show, not to speak of the criss-cross converse of a myriad mouths.

I came to the main intersection and amidst it all gazed towards an immense tree, which over the years had become a living landmark in the town. In the half-light, its gnarled old trunk twisted grimly upwards into a maze of branch and foliage,

73

reaching heavily into the night sky. Creepers hung down like mutilated cobwebs through the massive boughs, giving it a sense of increased antiquity amongst the corrugated iron roofs of Tenom. Unceasingly, the crowds were moving to and fro, but I noticed as they came to the tree, some were lingering for a moment. Out and up from the tangle of legs and arms and the sea of heads came the strains of an accordion. Was this some sideshow that their eyes had missed or some new sales stunt up from Jesselton? I could see that more were watching now, young students, native boys and then the older folk. I noticed one Chinese woman with her baby strapped to her back, its head a-nodding. All at once singing broke out, and someone stood on a box and began to speak. He was talking about Jesus Christ. They were truly my kinsmen standing there, Christians of Borneo telling their own people of the Treasure that no money can buy and only faith can grasp. I listened to their singing rising above the murmur of the crowds. It took on its true significance in such a circumstance, and set my heart on fire. It cut to the very core of the darkness and put the stab of ultimate life into the tawdry turbulence of the *Tamu*. I can hear it yet . . .

"What a wonderful change in my life has been wrought
Since Jesus came into my heart."

Some few days previously I had been with these same young Christians deep into the forest. It had proved the wildest of afternoons. We had hired Land-Rovers and scrambling aboard, some fifteen to twenty of us had driven several miles out of town into the country. Cutting in off the road we lumbered up and down over a dry mud track, until we plunged into heavy grass almost as high as the windscreen. Calling a halt by a rustic shelter we left the vehicles and proceeded 'safari' style to the fringe of the forest. At first we were obstructed by large numbers of felled rubber trees. An old plantation was being cut down to make way, no doubt, for fresh planting—but once this was negotiated, the foreboding forest loomed ahead.

74

To anyone who has never been into an 'equatorial evergreen rain forest', as my old geography master insisted on calling it, the experience is never to be forgotten.

The mere semblance of a path led in amongst the trees and almost immediately, both the sky above and the plantation behind, were lost to view. A sense of gloom and eerie dampness enveloped us and we began to move on rather automatically, pressed in by a hostile, menacing world of green. The narrow track, frighteningly overgrown, turned hither and thither. Jumping over fallen trees and rotting pieces of timber, we skirted the thorn-covered lower growth. Sometimes great buttress roots of a giant tree protruded in our way like the tailpiece of a rocket with a warhead in the leaves above. We were in constant danger of falling headlong, for the path was covered with decaying vegetation, wet and slippery, and vines and tendrils trailed everywhere. I was constantly on the alert. The slightest rustle in the undergrowth and I was sure a snake would dart away. As I put my foot down into the brushwood I wondered if some poisoned fang would sink into my ankle. I thought of the whole party now scattering carefree through the great forest away off the path, lost from view and piercing the dreadful silence with their shrieks and yells. Would we ever get out together alive—what if we lost someone, or one of the party suffered snake bite? On we walked deeper and deeper. The distance seemed interminable. How far should we go? Gradually the path disappeared and we crossed a stream and began to climb. Suddenly there was a scream in the forest—whatever had happened? It turned out to be nothing more than a leech on one of the girl's legs, determined to take its fill. As we increased our elevation we began to break clear of the bigger trees and come to more open ground. It was a relief to move into the light again. A short respite and we decided to drop down once more into the depths, get back to the stream, and then after a little more exploring, follow it down to the valley and the plantation. Our party was very scattered now and showing fatigue, but most of us reached the river bed. We ploughed our way up through the cool, shallow

75

water in a lather of sweat—ragged, dirty and breathless, hoping to reach the waterfall, which we believed must now be near at hand. Some of the boys were familiar with the forest life and to see them shin up a tree, lie along a slender branch and hang on until near breaking point, was astounding. They were enjoying it and gradually we, who were novices, enjoyed it too.

The afternoon wore on and there were still several of us trailing up through the water-course. We had reached just about our farthest point when suddenly one of the young people lunged forward with a shout. "The flower!" she cried. The young voice rang out in the stillness. I looked and there I saw a huge boulder set athwart the stream. It was lit by a shaft of light coming down between the trees and in a small cleft on the crown of the rock, lifting its head in quiet dignity, was a white orchid bursting into bloom.

It was an unforgettable moment, a moment of sheer purity in all the darkness of the forest. . . .

Thus I stood at the Tenom cross-roads amongst the *Tamu* crowds. We were no longer in the forest now, at least not in that one. We were amongst the people, and here were these same young men and women, full of vigour and strong in faith, venturing along another path. All around was this other jungle, the hazard of an entrenched and tangled superstition, harbouring the serpent's venom and the piercing thorn.

I often muse upon that small but triumphant group preaching Christ amongst the many there at Tenom, and when I do, there rises in me that shout amongst the trees—The flower! The flower!

Is there any more eloquent a symbol of the Church in the forest of the pagan world than that orchid, white and pure?

I think not, for this is Seed Eternal sown and brought to bloom by the very power of God.

CHAPTER ELEVEN

SUNSHINE BREAKING THROUGH

Men see not the bright light which is in the clouds. Elihu
*Behold, He cometh with clouds; and every eye shall
see Him.* John

A PIECE of paper lay on my desk. There was, of course, nothing
unusual in that. The study was a place of incessant activity, in
fact it was a kind of terminus for innumerable pieces of paper
moving in from Indonesia, Sarawak, Brunei and many a place
in North Borneo itself. It was the headquarters of a 'Correspondence—Bible School'. "Would you send me a photo of the
school?" one student had written. I could not help but smile.
Institutions certainly cannot be judged by their installations.
The school headquarters, namely my study, was one room. It
contained one table at which there was one chair. Apart from a
few rough bookcases fighting a losing battle against wood-worm
and silver-fish, a large cupboard for stocking Bibles and some
boxes for 'courses', there was nothing to catch the eye. A large-
scale map of the immediate district indicating the *kampongs*,
rubber estates, marshland and jungle adorned the main wall and
various old photographs hung here and there. That really was
about all. From my desk I looked out of the window to the
nextdoor gardens with their orchids and oleanders, whilst immediately below was the adjacent swampy field, where the
cheeky but lovable ragamuffins of the neighbourhood delighted
to catch tadpoles.

One day as I was marking the Scripture lessons I came to this
particular piece of paper. I stopped and looked at it closely. The
question ran, "What new thing are you willing for the Lord to
do for you?" The answer was set down in painstaking Chinese
characters and 'drawn' in bright green ink. Each one was distinct
and clear as if written by a boy still at school. They were written,

too, in the traditional style, from the top to the bottom of the page and the columns progressing from right to left. Slowly I deciphered it, the literal translation into English forming in my mind as I scanned the characters. As the meaning crystallised I was aware that this was not so much a student's answer, but a man's heart. The reply appealed to me as being unusually full of pathos and spiritual grace. "Without stopping," it ran, "I think in prayer, hoping in future for some new thing—willing for Him, in the place where there is no way, to open a way. Willing that He, in future, may have a plan of glory for me that will surpass all past glory. Willing that His lovingkindness should not cease towards me. Indeed His compassions are new every morning . . ."

"Do you think you could make a basket?" Nan asked. Hua-Kai-Yun looked somewhat taken aback. "Make a basket?" Why, he had never made a basket in his life. With a wry look on his face he dismissed the whole idea as totally impossible.

"You could make one, you know," persisted my wife, with all the insistence of an occupational therapist. Hua Kai Yun, taken by surprise, had no arguments ready to oppose the gentle art of basketry, other than his own inability.

"You can learn if you try. The others are doing it. Look at Ah-Soong there, he's made quite a lot. Come on now, you simply *must* have a try."

At the back of the T.B. wards of the General Hospital, where the grounds sloped away into an old rubber plantation, there was a little hut. One look inside and any unauthorised intruder would be amazed to see a stock of cane in various colours, together with an indescribable conglomeration of baskets. Plain baskets, fancy baskets, shopping baskets, waste-paper baskets, in fact almost any kind of basket you could think of. From this store-room Hua-Kai-Yun now received a quota of cane and under the enthusiastic, if not too expert instruction of his fellow patients, he began the intricate operation of making his very first basket. He would be paid for his efforts from the funds of

N.O.B.A.T.A.[1] It would only mean about fifty cents but to him this would represent his first earnings for several years. Just to be able to do a job of work, he was going to discover, would be almost better than a dose of medicine, but he had never thought of it that way before.

Slowly he worked. How clumsy his fingers seemed and the cane so unyielding. "I'm too ill to do this," he kept thinking. Three long years had passed since he was admitted, and had come in up through the narrow driveway, past the broad lawns and the shrubs filled with yellow flowers to the neat little T.B. compound. It was a secluded sanctuary. A real haven of healing and convalescence. The staff were very kind and the doctors so helpful, but he did not really improve and he felt that his youth had already slipped away. If it had not been that he belonged to Christ, life would have lost all its meaning long ago. He knew without question that God loved him and cared for him as a Father, but with his weakening frame and tired mind there were some days when he felt he could hardly carry on any more. It was little wonder, after all the hazardous and strenuous years.

Hua-Kai-Yun had been born on Hainan Island off the south coast of China, in a poor farming family some years before the last war. He could remember the quiet and placid days of his boyhood. Summer days when white fleecy clouds would fleck the blue expanse above and sunshine chase the shadows in the paddy fields below. Perhaps that was the reason they had called him Hua-Kai-Yun, which means the 'sunshine breaking through'. All his family were people of the fields and there had always been a struggle to make two ends meet. Nevertheless they had known the rare contentment of simple pleasures which few but the poor enjoy.

He was only fourteen years of age when the first Japanese bombers came strafing in from the sea. His school-house was reduced to rubble by one of the very first bombs. Then the aggressor armies invaded and terror spread through the country-side, as town after town was occupied by the enemy forces.

[1] North Borneo Anti-Tuberculosis Association.

79

When they eventually reached his village, his house was cruelly burnt to the ground and his old grandmother done to death. The whole family scattered. His mother unable to face the bitter privations, fell ill and having no medical aid, died very quickly. Hua-Kai-Yun thus found himself alone with his older sister, fighting for his life and hers, amongst the widespread ruins. Once his sister was sixteen it was possible for her to get married and in some measure this was a way of escape for her but it meant, of course, that Hua-Kai-Yun was left 'empty' and alone. "I was like a sheep that had lost its way and like a small boat drifting on the great ocean. What could I do? Where could I go?" That was his own description of his plight.

Mercifully he came in contact with a relative at this time, an aunt, who took him in and did her best for him. By making various contacts and arrangements, even in the upheaval of the times, it proved possible for Hua-Kai-Yun to board a vessel bound for North Borneo. His father had left, some years previously, for those parts, seeking a better livelihood. No doubt he could establish contact and live with his father. It was a big venture but it succeeded, and for some while he and his father worked together on a plantation near Tawau. The tropical climate, however, proved too much for Hua-Kai-Yun, and it was not long before he contracted malaria and succumbed to a foot disease which gave him excruciating pain. As Borneo was also occupied by the Japanese at that time, it was not until after the liberation that he was able to get medical treatment. This proved to be reasonably successful and he was able, in the goodness of God, to move to Sandakan and obtain employment in a café. Although physically weakened by work in the plantation under occupation conditions, God was obviously undertaking for him. In Sandakan he had his first contact with the Gospel.

"In the summer of 1948," he confided, "I came to know Our Lord Jesus Christ through the witness of a Chinese preacher in Sandakan. It happened like this. One day whilst working in the tea-shop a Chinese gentleman came in, sat down and ordered some tea. I was conscious that he was looking at me rather intently. After quite a while he took, what proved to be a picture, out of his pocket and said to me, 'Do you know who this is?' " Hua-Kai-Yun was undoubtedly mystified.

Without waiting for a reply, the gentleman said quietly but with obvious enthusiasm, "That man was born at Bethlehem and He died at a place called Golgotha, nailed to a wooden cross. Because He shed His blood there, your sins can be forgiven." Hua-Kai-Yun was even more baffled. The man quoted quite a number of sentences from a book called the Bible and then said, "Why don't you come along to our little chapel and we can explain more about these things to you?"

Hua-Kai-Yun did not know what to think but he was intrigued by such an encounter with one of the customers and found himself impatiently watching the clock on the wall, waiting for the time when he would slip away to the chapel. Before the time came, however, the Chinese gentleman reappeared and escorted Hua-Kai-Yun all the way.

"He took me," Hua-Kai-Yun related, "through several side streets to a rather unfrequented part of the town where there was a house built of wooden planks and roofed with *atap*. We walked inside and I saw twenty to thirty people already sitting in the rows of chairs. I was asked to sit in the middle of the first row. As I looked around I realised that none of those present were known to me and I rather felt that they were looking at me. After a few minutes we were all asked to sing. I had no idea what I was supposed to do, so I just stood up with the others. After the singing the Chinese gentleman preached for some time, then everyone stood up again and closed their eyes whilst the preacher quietly spoke a few words. I was amazed and very disturbed, looking this way and that to see what they would do until they had opened their eyes again. When all was over the preacher bade me farewell in a very friendly way and asked me to come again the next week."

As these different occasions came and went a new faith began to spring up in Hua-Kai-Yun and with it, a new hope. The strange encounter in the tea-shop took on a special significance and as Hua-Kai-Yun heard more of the Man who was born at Bethlehem and who died at Golgotha, he came to know Him as his very own Saviour and Lord.

Continuing his story, Hua-Kai-Yun went on, "One night when I arrived back at the tea-shop after attending one of the meetings, I was confronted by my 'boss'. He stood behind the counter and fixing his dark, black eyes upon me, exploded with anger. 'If you think you can leave the shop for two or three hours at a time, then you are mistaken,' he growled. 'You're just robbing me right and left, that's what you're doing. The bit of work you do, doesn't even cover your wages. What do you expect to gain going off like that? Now I'm just not going to have it. I tell you now—any more trouble and that's you without a job! Do you understand?' "

Hua-Kai-Yun, weak in body and more or less alone in the world, was no match for his hard-hearted and ruthless employer. He felt he could only bow his head to the grindstone and plod on. Years passed and he was unable to attend any Christian service and unable to fortify himself with any Christian fellowship. He felt his new-found faith was dwindling away.

At last in 1954 he obtained fresh employment, this time in Jesselton the capital, but it was too late, his health was already seriously impaired. The daily exertion and long hours proved too much for him and eventually he contracted tuberculosis. At first the illness responded to treatment but in the end he could work no longer and he had to be admitted to the T.B. hospital. So it was that we met him there and had our visits with him from time to time, seeking to be of encouragement and help to him.

How many must there be like him in Southeast Asia. Broken and battered, blasted from their homes, bereft of their loved ones, cast out on the refuse heap of a diseased and dispossessed humanity. On they go, stumbling and falling, eking out any kind of living, anywhere and in any circumstance, until their emaciated bodies will move no longer and their meagre labour can be exploited no more.

Hua-Kai-Yun by God's grace is weathering the storm. He will never be a basket-maker, but his faith, nourished by regular Bible study and refreshed in fellowship, has like some smoking flax been kindled once again to a living flame.

I looked down at my desk. There on the table was the piece of paper, where Hua-Kai-Yun's Chinese characters stood out boldly in the bright green ink. "What new thing are you willing for the Lord to do for you?" ran the question. How great was the answer of this man, called so aptly, 'Sunshine breaking through' . . .

"Without stopping, I think in prayer, hoping in future for some new thing—willing for Him, in the place where there is no way, to open a way. Willing that He, in future, may have a plan of glory for me that will surpass all past glory. Willing that His lovingkindness should not cease towards me. Indeed His compassions are new every morning . . ."

CHAPTER TWELVE

A HIGHWAY FOR THE WIDOW

The silver is mine, and the gold is mine, saith the Lord of Hosts.
Haggai

PRISCILLA sat in her little brown house situated on the outskirts of the seafaring town of Sandakan. Out in the harbour the native boats plied to and fro and the sun fell brightly on the verdant hills beyond the urban fringe. Down in the market and along the sidewalks business was much the same as usual. You could catch the rattle of an abacus as you passed the Chinese shops and the shouting of the coolies out on the wharf. In quieter moments you could hear the fresh lap of the waves or the laughter of the children down the street. For a few harsh seconds would come the screech of a ship's horn or, in the stillness above, the plaintive cry of a gull, flying in from the sea. Each day, no doubt, was much the same as any other, there on the harbour front of Sandakan.

Yet for Priscilla this was her darkest day, a day of bitterness, more bitter than she had ever known. Her mind was altogether numbed with grief; her heart a pent up reservoir of tears.

Wistfully her fingers fondled the slender yellow thread still hanging from her neck. "Can it be thirty years," she thought, "since I twined these soft white strands and dipped them in the yellow dye? Those surely were the days of a young girl's dream, a dream which all came true." How quickly the wedding day had dawned and that golden thread been placed about her neck. From then on she had begun to wear the sari and, of course, from that day until now, the little yellow cord had never left her, for she was a wife amongst the Indian community.

Slowly her fingers came to rest on the tiny gilt cross and diminutive Bible which formed the graceful pendulant to the yellow strand. She remembered how her Christian father-in-law had been most adamant that the Hindu cord should be adorned with these appendages. She had never thought about them very much. Religion, whether of one kind or another, had little meaning for Priscilla, especially today.

How hard it suddenly seemed to remove it; to lift it up over the head; to reverse that precious movement of three decades ago; to tell the world that death had dissolved that union. Such was the custom for an Indian woman in Borneo and Priscilla knew that there was no other way for the widow; no other way for her.

Time and again within herself she would be stealing away to the hospital and in her grief-torn mind each detail of the last sad scene would be relived. Must death be so dreadful, so final, so cruel? Now she was alone, yet not completely. There were the children but then they had their own affairs; and some were hardly children now. She thought of Lois for a moment, and her first boy-friend. How different everything was from her young days. Yes, they would soon forget and she would always be alone. Yet she must not forget that sweet Karen Christian who, with her husband, had shown her a kindness that seemed to bring the great God very near. There was consolation in their companionship and Someone very close when they prayed in Jesus' Name. And that was the strange thing on that last day, when nearly all the family were gathered at the bedside. "Do you know how to pray?" she had asked him. Strange that she, Priscilla, should say that! He had not spoken a word in answer but simply drawn a cross upon his forehead with his fingers. Then she had sat and looked at him, so weak there in his bed, until she began to cry. "I'll not die," he had gasped, but even as he spoke he had started to breathe more heavily. Oxygen was quickly brought and as it was administered he revived again. For a long while she and the children had lingered, tenderly watching him, then he had done what Indians always do when the world of shadows closes in. "Bring me some milk," he asked. The nurse came quickly and taking it from her hand he drank a little, then passed it on to Priscilla. Whenever he did this, she had known what he implied. She sipped it and passed it then to Sundar.

Trancelike, the young man took it, sipping the glass as his mother had done before him, then passed it on to Junia. When all had taken their turn, her husband had seemed content, becoming very quiet and still. Slowly the eyes began to close until the long black lashes kissed each other for the last time. The windows were darkened now, she felt. He will never speak again.

Sundar looked at his father incredulously. "He's not dead," he said deliberately. "I won't believe he's dead. He's only sleeping!" But she, Priscilla, his wife for thirty years, had known instinctively that the cord of life was broken. Her beloved had passed the unknown frontier to the world beyond . . .

Suddenly there was a knock at the door. Priscilla roused herself from her sad reverie, rose to her feet and, walking slowly across the wooden floor, opened it. She was confronted by a Chinese gentleman. 'What could his business be?' she cautiously wondered. Contrary to the usual formalities and approaches of the Orient he spoke to her quite directly, in fact too directly for Priscilla's liking. She was in no mood to discuss her affairs with strangers. "I was wondering," said the Chinese gentleman, "whether perhaps, in view of your husband's death you were considering selling your plot of land, which I understand you still hold in Sandakan. I would pay ready cash of course. Perhaps in the circumstances this might prove of help to you." He waited for the desired effect and then continued. "The figure I have in mind is round about fifteen hundred dollars, although seeing you are a widow I would be prepared to go to two thousand if necessary." "Two thousand dollars." The words began to sink into Priscilla's mind. What a help this would be, especially now that her husband's pension was not to be paid to her. How could people be so unkind, she thought. Even while his body was yet lying in the house, someone had come in and said, "What a foolish man your husband was to alter his contract with the authorities! If he hadn't done that, you would be all right now." Such words had only rubbed salt into the open wound of bereavement. Why can't people think when they speak? Two thousand dollars in her hand now! Without doubt it could solve a lot—but Priscilla hesitated. Some intuitive sense restrained her. It was as if some-one was telling her, "Don't agree to it! You are *not* to agree to it." Looking at the stranger she said, "I'll think about it." It was as well she did. Two thousand dollars was barely half the value of the holding concerned.

During those days Priscilla was just a sitting prey for any un-scrupulous dealer who might come along. They knew her plight. They knew that she would be obliged to vacate the government quarters that she and her family occupied. They knew she must be in need. How could she go on? How could she fight alone, a world so callous and so cash-conscious? There was no one to guard or guide her; no one to take the decisions now; no one in whom to confide; no one with whom to take counsel. How precarious the lot of a widow cast out into a heathen world. She looked at their little home. It was hard to believe that even this must be dismantled now, and what of the little ones? The older children could fend for themselves but the smaller children needed her and once her meagre capital was spent what could she give them to eat? She was no longer a young woman. What work could she find that would solve her problems?

Gradually, but relentlessly, the burden mounted until the whole thing became utterly insupportable. If she could have cried she would have done so but her heart was too tense even for tears.

It was during one of these shadowed moments of grief and fear that the beloved Karen Christian called again. She was like a ray of sunshine coming into the gloom and Priscilla wondered at her love for her. Today she brought a text, beautifully drawn and tastefully framed. Together they hung it up on the wall. Priscilla looked at the words. She had never read them be-fore.

"Thou art the Helper of the fatherless," it ran. "You must pray," said the Karen lady. "You *must* pray. There is nothing you can do about it all now. It is no good sitting and brooding

87

over everything; and if you just sit and mope you will get no-where." It sounded so matter of fact, almost brusque, but there was kindliness behind the firmness of those words. Of course it was true. She must face it. Life must go on but what her dear friend was saying was simply this, "You need not face it alone. There *is* a Helper."

One day some eight months later we drove the car in off the Tuaran road, just outside Jesselton, and looking this way and that amongst the bungalows, located at last, one newly painted not very far ahead. The drive-way was rather overgrown with grass but the garden showed signs of recent care and here and there young trees and shrubs had been planted. We tumbled out of the car, clambered up the stairway and found ourselves standing on a little raised patio, bordered with flowerpots containing healthy-looking plants. The front door was open and we were welcomed in by Lois and Junia. It was a lovely place, spacious, airy and suitably furnished. We sat down in the comfortable turquoise-coloured chairs. Against the wall opposite the window were some shelves containing ornaments, the most beautiful of which were two examples of tree coral. The natural tracery of the formation was exquisite. How delicate and tender the hands of the Fashioner must be. Above the shelves there was the treasured text set in a place of prominence for all to see.

"Thou art the Helper of the fatherless."

A few moments passed and Priscilla, dressed in her long sari, swept quietly into the room. It was the first time I had ever seen her. All I can say is that her face was Christian. Her fine Indian features were set in a serene and open countenance. There was the light of a triumphant faith in her eyes. Her whole face seemed to epitomise that meek and quiet spirit which the Bible tells us is of great price in the sight of God. I wondered how it all happened. I had come in order to hear about her faith for she wished to be baptised—but I hardly needed to converse with her. She was already in the Master's hands.

We talked just a little while and then she began to confide in

us. "The house," she explained, "was fifteen thousand dollars."
Normally this would have been purely her personal business but
for her it was something quite different. It represented to her not
a human transaction but a miracle of God. She was really trying
to say in these figures, "You see how God cares. You see how
He is a Helper to the fatherless."

In her deep distress those months ago, at her wits end and without resources, she had decided to give the Christians' God His
chance. If He cared then let Him be pleased to show His care.
That is how she felt. Her attitude had hardly been faith and yet
it was not exactly unbelief. If He would prove Himself to her,
then she would trust herself to Him, so she had begun to pray.
In a way it was all on a rather low level of spiritual experience.
She was perhaps rather like Jacob or even Hannah, both of
whom said "If Thou wilt. . . . I will," but when God sees that
we are going to take Him at His Word, He is always ready to take
us at our word. It is this that surprises us and Priscilla had been
surprised beyond measure. The first real inkling that God was
with her had been the receiving of a grant from the Government
of some nine thousand dollars in view of her husband's service.
This was substantial and gave her time to give proper consideration to her plot of land in Sandakan. Eventually she made
proper application under the Land Regulations to sell the land.
Then the house in the Jesselton area became available and she
decided to go a step farther in this question of trusting God. If
her large family were to be rehoused then this was undoubtedly
the house for them but the sizeable figure of fifteen thousand
dollars was the lowest price the owner would consider. She
determined therefore to gather her family around her and to
make a convenant with God. Thus they prayed together, saying
in utter simplicity something like this. "Dear God, if you will
give us five thousand dollars for the land in Sandakan then we
will truly believe you and we will all become Christians." In
view of the original offer of only two thousand dollars this was a
large petition. Five thousand dollars was the minimum amount
which, with their other funds in hand, would make the purchase

of the Jesselton house possible. If God was for them, then He could do the impossible thing.

Having settled the matter in her heart she now went resolutely about her business. The full sum of fifteen thousand must be paid by April 30th or the offer would be withdrawn. Could God meet such requirements? Was there such a thing as an abacus in heaven? Did God deal in the currency of North Borneo? It was hard to believe—but the text said, He was a Helper to the fatherless, and does not the Christian's God mean what He says? The next indication that God was moving on their behalf came when a letter from the authorities arrived, saying that the sale of the land had been authorised and the necessary documents could be obtained from the local court. Joyfully, Priscilla made her way to the appropriate office in Jesselton to obtain the papers but she came hard up against her first disappointment. The magistrate was away at Tawau and it would be ten days before the papers could be issued. A week later she called again. No, the magistrate had not yet returned. "Come again tomorrow," she was told. The next day she retraced her steps. It was hot and the journey particularly tiring. This time the judge had returned but naturally had many matters to deal with and it proved impossible to obtain the papers that day either. Precious time was now slipping away. Why this unexpected delay? Tomorrow would be almost the last day that the documents would avail her. The date-line for settlement of the house purchase was dangerously near. The following morning she returned to the office. Again she received a setback. Once again she was told to come tomorrow. She could bear it no longer. "My legs are tired," she said. "I will wait till nightfall if only you will give me the papers." That afternoon the papers were completed, and duly signed, and now she was legally entitled to negotiate the sale of the plot and complete the transaction whenever she wished. Almost immediately she wired her son Sundar, in Sandakan. Within a matter of hours a telegram came back. "Offered $2000." Her heart fell a little. Still only two thousand. Was she really asking the impossible? Almost before she had time to repudiate this first offer, another telegram arrived. "Offered $2800." She held her ground and wired back a refusal. This was no longer a matter of dollars nor even of a home for her children. This was a question as to whether God existed or not. Whether Christ was real or not. Whether prayer to the Living God was mockery or not. She would take not a dollar under five thousand. As she stiffened in her determination and faith, another telegram arrived. There had been a big leap forward. "Offered $4000." She was amazed. The original offer had now been doubled, but she felt absolutely under bond not to accept it. It would have seemed extraordinary to anyone else. Was she right to gamble her family and faith like this? But she had made a covenant with God. After a pause, a more or less final figure of four thousand eight hundred was put forward. An excellent price. Surely no one could expect more for the particular piece of land in question. Was it not the right, and indeed the very best thing, to accept this offer immediately? It was only two hundred dollars short, anyway, of her ideal price, her convenant price. Was it not enough? Priscilla did not think so. She was determined now to go all the way with God. Quietly she awaited the final development. Would one more telegram come? It did. She was not to be disappointed. She held the envelope in her hand a moment. Strange that a figure, a mere price, should be the last factor in her total surrender to Jesus Christ. She opened it and saw just what she had expected to see. "Offered $5000", the message ran. It was enough. From that moment she believed, from that moment she belonged to Him, to God, to Christ who long ago had paid the other price, the price of sin. O Matchless God—Helper of the Fatherless— Saviour of all who dare to trust Him!

On the morning of the baptism Priscilla arrived at the believers meeting hall dressed in a flowing white sari. For her this was a stupendous moment. As a child she had been brought up in an idolatrous Hindu home. She could remember distinctly the pictures of 'the goddess with many hands' all over the walls of her home and how her father and mother used to burn incense and light the lamp in veneration of this mysterious personage. She could recall how they would bow down to the floor in abject worship of this paper goddess. Today she was to go down into the waters of baptism publicly confessing her faith in Christ. Forty and more years previously, as a young child, she had attended the opening celebrations of the Sikh temple just down the road. All she could remember now was seeing the big sacred cow and a large book, together with two men holding feather fans who kept fanning the cow, whilst others prayed to it. That was what she had been born to believe but now she had been *born again* and today she had come in a symbolic way to bury the past and tell everyone that she would walk with Jesus in newness of life. After the burial of her husband Priscilla had felt she would never smile again but God had now filled her heart with singing.

As I looked at her that morning I wondered really whether it was practical to baptise her in her long sari so I asked her, "How do you wish to be baptised?" "Just as I am," she replied. That is how she had come to the Saviour and that is how she confessed him. When the moment came there was something strangely moving about this Christian Indian lady. She had been through much but she knew with all her heart that she believed in Jesus Christ, the Son of God. Stately and serene she descended into the water. I questioned her, as I had done the other converts. "Do you believe on the Lord Jesus Christ as your own personal Saviour?" "I do," she said. Thus one more of Asia's children owned the sway of Jesus Christ. Following her one by one into the water came her three older daughters, Junia, Lois and Lydia. They were not afraid of their family covenant. God had kept his Word and should they not keep theirs?

CHAPTER THIRTEEN

DUSUN HORIZON

I say to this man, Go, and he goeth: and to another, Come,
and he cometh: and to my servant, Do this, and he doeth it.
Matthew

DARKNESS had long since fallen and it was nearly bedtime, when suddenly there was a sharp knock on the wooden door. Who could it be? I turned the handle and cautiously drew the door open. There stood Nat, tense and speechless, his figure lit up by the electric light, and waiting to come in. As I greeted him I became suddenly aware that the purpose of his call was unusual. He said little and we moved quickly through the living-room into the study.

What could have happened? His young Chinese face was more squarely set that night. The youth was plainly over-wrought and I wondered what I could do for him. Settling him in one of the wicker chairs I looked across, feeling sympathetic yet curious, and waiting for him to lay down his burden.

He was only twenty-one, but the gold on his teeth and his rather prominent features gave him at times a look beyond his years. I gazed into his dark brown eyes and as I did so, I could see that they were filling with hot passionate tears. Why was he so upset? Normally he was one of the happiest of all the young Christians in Jesselton. I waited patiently, but his own emotion kept back his words.

At last he blurted out in a heart-broken way, "They want me to go back to Singapore. My father says I ought to go back there and help my young brother in his education." I listened, trying hard to analyse the nature of the crisis in Nat's troubled mind. There must be more to it than this. Piece by piece the whole story came out. He was training as a teacher in Jesselton and was in the middle of his course. To break off now would ruin his career and almost certainly put an end to his studies, but it was not the question of his career which disturbed Nat. It was his vocation. The question was not what he, as a man wanted to do, but what God was telling him to do. As a Chinese he felt a sense of deep loyalty to his parents, yet as a Christian he felt also a binding obligation to God. Could he not please both the Father above and the father below? For the first time in his young life he faced a conflict of loyalties that seemed impossible to resolve. How could he be a traitor to his family? Did he not owe everything to them? Yet how could he betray his Redeemer and the destiny to which he was called? In the last analysis did he not owe everything rather to Him who died and rose again? Who can measure the burnings of a heart once set aflame by the love of Christ? As I listened to him it was hard to penetrate beyond the tears to the heart's own story.

It was the natives that concerned him. A year or two back His Royal Highness the Duke of Edinburgh had paid a visit to the Colony. There had been many celebrations, the most outstanding of which had been an extensive exhibition of the culture, customs and crafts of the native peoples of North Borneo. "It was there," Nat said, "when the *padang* near the shore were thronging with the Dusuns, the Muruts and many others, that God spoke to me. I was made acutely aware of their spiritual darkness. In those days I pondered deeply their way of life. I looked at their simple clothes, their primitive dwellings, their sinister superstitions and a great surge filled my heart. I felt that God was calling me to devote my life to these lovable yet needy peoples."

So strong was this urge upon him that he wrote a little later to an older Christian in Singapore, confiding in him the secret yearnings of his soul. In May 1959, he told him, "My future in North Borneo is not at all bright, when looked at from an earthly point of view. I may not be able to be trained in the official college here but my aim is not merely to obtain a recognised certificate but rather to be sent to the schools in the remote villages where I could bring the Good News to the natives. I hope that I will be sent there following my two year training period."

In the August of the same year it was evident that God was still working in his heart. Writing to his friend again Nat said, "I have prayed hard . . . and I am convinced that I should continue here in Borneo. I want to struggle on. In His strength I want to glorify His Name in North Borneo. My lot is with the natives who have not heard the glorious Good News! . . . I am persuaded that 'God shall direct my paths'."

The following month Nat reached a new peak of dedication. He wrote, "I know He is leading me step by step. The proverb declares, 'as thou goest, step by step I will open up the way before thee'. He promises to lead, so I commit my life into His Hand. I yield my life a living sacrifice unto God, for this is my reasonable service. Pray brother, that I should not disobey Him and should not count my life precious to myself."

This was the background of the conflict. At the particular juncture at which he now stood he felt to make arrangements for a permanent return to Singapore would be a betrayal of a God-appointed mission, yet to write to his father and tell him the facts was almost more than he could do. The more he pondered the matter, the greater the sense of impasse. How could he face his father if he failed the family? How could he face his God if he failed to obey the call? So as he knocked on the door and now sat in the study he found himself on the verge of tears. What Nat had not yet understood but was soon to learn was this, that where there is the Will of God there is always the Way of God.

We had a long conversation together and a time of quiet waiting upon the Lord. His heart was stilled. He would write now to his father and put all before him, not over-riding his wishes but confiding in him as a son. Naturally speaking, it was not feasible to expect that his father would change his mind. There was everything to militate against this, but Nat must know that God can never use us in self-will. We must be still and let God do the impossible in answer to our prayer of faith. To write such a letter to his father, who hardly shared his Christian beliefs, seemed only to invite an even more adamant insistence that he should return to Singapore, but God *is* able to work *all* things after the counsel of His own will. Nat was now prepared to trust to God alone in this. His Father on high would not fail him. A few weeks later Nat came to the house again. This time there were no tears in his eyes unless they were tears of joy. The unbelievable had happened. A letter from his father revealed a complete reversal of his previous outlook. Nat had been given full liberty to complete his studies in Borneo. As to the more distant future, the God, who had led thus far could be wholly relied upon to complete His purpose. . . .

It was eight-thirty in the morning and the hills were still head and neck in a muffler of white cloud but Nat had risen early and now, with a Dusun boy called Jack, was heading for the Keningau road. Nat had looked forward very much to this trip. It was his holiday time and he felt the days could hardly be better spent than making an exploratory trip into the Borneo interior. In his diary he noted with student-like efficiency:

Trip to the Interior Towns

Purpose: To obtain a first-hand knowledge of the natives.

(*a*) *Their surroundings;*
(*b*) *Their way of life;*
(*c*) *Their spiritual need.*

He and the boy were travelling light and with the help of old bicycles, hoped to traverse quite a few miles each day along the gravel roads and bridle paths linking the small communities, thirty to fifty miles inland from the west coast.

Nat had little idea just how exacting and even hazardous the journey before him would prove. The intense heat, the overgrown paths, the inadequate transport, the native bridges and jungle rivers were to try him to the utmost. His plan was quite ambitious. His route was to start from Tenom and take in Keningau, Tambunan, Kirakot, Ranau and then, by skirting

Mount Kinabalu, to make a return journey via Tamporuli to Jesselton. For this exacting schedule he had optimistically set himself a limit of just nine days!

The first leg of the journey gave them their initial taste of the dust and dirt of a sunbaked gravel road. Every passing jeep enveloped them in a cloud of choking sand and the miles seemed longer and longer as the sun climbed higher in the sky. After the first seventeen to twenty miles the rubber plantations gave way to more evident forest growth. Soon the huge trees of the rain forests with their buttress roots could be seen from the road and they passed three barefooted Dusun natives clad in dirty tattered shirts and short black trousers, each clutching a catapult. After 'Mile Twenty-six', however, there were numerous native houses built near to the road and the land round about these dwellings was well planted with tapioca, coconut and *rambutan*.[1] Whenever the terrain of the land permitted, the Dusuns had planted rice fields.

It was with great relief that they pulled in to a *kampong* some two miles outside of Keningau. As they approached one of the compounds they saw a Dusun woman carrying a length of thick bamboo some five feet long. Jack explained to Nat that this was the way the people carried water. The hollow bamboo, once the nodes are pierced, makes an excellent light-weight container. The gate of the compound was also made of bamboo, three or four bamboo poles being placed in suitable slots in two wooden posts some few feet apart. Negotiating the gate they were welcomed by a hospitable Dusun family for the night. The houses were built on poles, whilst the walls and stairway were made of planks and the roof from *atap*. The flooring was comprised of a great number of long, thin slats of bamboo placed close together, the shiny surface making it smooth for the sole of the foot. Walls dividing the rooms were similarly constructed. Nat was very conscious of the primitive character of the people's way of life. Hardly anyone could read either Kadazan[2] or Malay and there

[1] *Rambutan*—from *rambut*—Malay for 'beard'. It is a red hairy fruit with a juicy grape-like centre.   [2] Kadazan—the language of the Dusun people.

was obviously a great ignorance of hygiene. All were pagans given to the worship of demons which they believed to haunt the countryside. At evening time, numerous friends came in from neighbouring houses and two big, round jars of *tapai*[1] were placed on the floor, one amongst the women and one amongst the men, who tended to sit in two separate groups. A small stick of bamboo was thrust into each jar and throughout the evening the jars, together with the stick were passed from one to another. The Dusuns drank far into the night. The only food that accompanied the *tapai* was scraps of beef. The Dusuns are normally a kindly and peace-loving people but the *tapai* tends to make them querulous and then fighting is not uncommon.

The next morning Nat woke up to find that a hill mist limited visibility to about half a mile. It was a new experience for him. He enjoyed a native breakfast of onion fried in oil and water, some fried beef and also some local vegetables fried in oil and curry. Once breakfast was over Nat and the Dusun boy started off with light hearts towards Tambunan on the next stage of their journey.

By 10.15 a.m. they managed to reach Apin Apin and after a brief visit to one of his pupils, who happened to live there, Nat and Jack left the small township to be confronted almost immediately by a difficult river. They struggled manfully through the flowing stream half carrying their bicycles and knee deep in water. Nat fell and almost received a ducking but he managed to get through, dry at least, from the waist up. On the farther bank were a party of Dusun natives taking their *kerbau*[2] to the Keningau market. Nat and Jack now pressed on until they reached Kitau, a 'haunted' village they were told, and then proceeded out along a lonely and ominous stretch of the track surrounded on all sides by immense trees. They were still sixteen miles from their destination. Suddenly Nat looked at his Dusun companion and he could see that the blood was draining from his dark skin giving him a strange pallid appear-

[1] Malay—*Tapai:* an alcoholic beverage made from fermented rice.
[2] Malay—*Kerbau:* buffalo.

ance. It was impossible to continue. Jack was feeling very ill and his temperature was obviously rising. They sat down. Unless some unexpected vehicle came along in that isolated spot it would mean a night alone in the forest. The prospect was unenviable and Nat instinctively turned in prayer to God spreading the whole circumstance before Him. In his diary he wrote down, with quiet confidence, *My trust is in God. He will provide the necessary help in His own time.* Half an hour went by and then to their unbounded joy, along came a jeep. Jack was lifted into the vehicle, together with his bicycle and the provisions. God had answered. Nat learned afterwards that this jeep was the last one on the road that day. It was now left for Nat to continue alone, the remaining distance into Tambunan. After a further nine miles he was exhausted. The path was little more than a jungle track. As he came to the banks of another river he was tempted to camp alone but all equipment had gone forward in the jeep. There were still six miles to go. The last few hours had proved the very toughest of the whole trip. He wondered how he would ever get through. The pressure of the solitude now bore in upon him. How dreadfully silent the forest; but he typically recorded, *I was not really alone. God was with me.* At 7.15 p.m. after trudging all day in relentless heat Nat staggered into Tambunan. Jack was in hospital. How the trip would go it was hard to tell. Nat found some accommodation in a schoolhouse and after a meal and a refreshing wash in a nearby stream he lay down to rest. Before going to sleep he opened his Bible and read a few verses from the New Testament. What did it say? "The world passeth away and the lust thereof: but he that doeth the will of God abideth forever."

There was no doubt in his mind, he must persevere. The trip must at all costs be carried through. By the following Monday Jack was sufficiently recovered from his fever to continue the journey and so day by day they moved on staying with Dusun folk whenever possible, in order that the purpose of the itineration might be fully realised. As they approached the Ranau district they ran into tall grass called *lalang*. This made the going exceedingly difficult. The grass cut the exposed parts of their skin and as they tried to ride their bikes along the narrow overgrown footway they were frequently thrown into the undergrowth. *"After a few miles of travelling in such conditions,"* Nat noted in his diary, *"we came to a fairly open space. Stretching away below us was a deep valley. The scenery was majestic and high up on the mountain slope I suddenly spotted a small native hut. Around it there was some hill-paddy. As I stood there, gazing up at it, I wondered, 'Have those people heard the Name of Jesus?' Simultaneously those last words of my Lord Jesus came back to me, 'Ye shall be witnesses unto me . . . unto the uttermost part of the earth.' Surely the Lord will never leave them out though they be so far away . . ."*

After another two or three days of arduous travelling, Nat managed to reach Jesselton. He had done what he had set out to do. It took him some eight days to recover but all this was but a step towards his destiny.

Had he not vowed, "My lot is with the natives who have not heard the Gospel"?

CHAPTER FOURTEEN

OLD SULIDAN, THE CHIEFTAIN

There came an old man from his work out of the field at
even ... and the old man said, Whither goest thou? And
whence comest thou? Judges

IN the flawless sunshine of the dawn the rugged head of Kinabalu rises in lofty grandeur from the steaming jungles thirteen
thousand feet below. Slowly the wakening giant draws to its
spreading girth, a golden cummerbund of cloud, and peers like
some imperious chieftain in naked majesty over the vast extent
of his domain. From the bare and glistening rock that forms the
summit beneath the dome of blue, the eye looks out to endless
forest and the far horizons of the southern seas.

From the murky shadows of the matted trees that wrap the
feet of Kinabalu in perennial gloom, the thoughts of native
men and women reach out unconsciously to the mountain.
Standing on the debris of a rough-hewn clearing or venturing
on some hunting expedition to the lower slopes, they look up to
this mighty Olympus of the Orient. To them, beyond the lifting
cloud and somewhere diffused throughout the halo-light of the
high serrated ridges, is found the dwelling of those gods and
demons that control the destinies of all the tribes.

If you follow the jungle paths out to the upland sweep of the
hills you will see, in the monsoon season, a myriad of rivulets filling
the furrowed approaches of the mountain. It would seem that
the rugged face of Kinabalu has chosen to water all the lowlands
with its tears. As the streams converge, the Tempasuk river,
known to the Dusuns as the Kadamayan, is slowly born. Moving
on to the coastal plains it slackens and then broadens. One by
one, it links the villages, as beads upon a raffia-thread, until it
meanders placidly through the pastures of Kota Belud to the
sea.

This was Sulidan's country. How he loved it, the rugged hinterland, the silent forest and the soft sweet green of the freshly planted paddy. He knew the trees, the many trails and the faces of his people. He could gauge the prowess of the braves and the 'two-hearts' of the schemers. Every headman must give account to him. No whisper beneath the trees, or affair of the *kampongs*, was allowed to escape his ear. When anger and jealousy threatened to disrupt his people, he knew the trouble-makers. The magic-men respected him and the selfish and the avaricious were aware of his impartial judgements, for was he not their acknowledged chieftain, the aged Sulidan?

With the advance of years a distressing deafness harassed the old man in his work of administration. The long conversations and the arbitrating of disputes became increasingly strenuous for him. Some, perhaps, began to wonder if his day was done, and that soon he must withdraw to the shadows of the community, waiting for the great darkness to descend. But although his ears might fail he could still listen with a heart that beat like a night-drum, in unison with the yearnings of his kindred . . .

On one particular day Sulidan sat in his hut built on poles and roofed with Sago-palm, engrossed in the making of a decision. His brown, quizzical face, creased and crinkled like an iguana's skin, looked more than usually ponderous. Today's decision was linked with something he had already decided some four months previously. The course he had adopted then, and which had already affected him profoundly, raised now this new and challenging situation, and he wanted to be absolutely right in what he was about to do. For many years he had been a ruler of men. There was little doubt some feared him, but then there were others who loved him. He was not afraid of men nor did he fear to rule over them. What perturbed him was the secret held within his own heart. The fact that the terror of the demon-world gripped him as the jaws of a crocodile grip its prey and drag it down to death. The thrust of a spear, the flight of an arrow, the dread piercing of a blow-pipe dart, he could understand. Such weapons had their safeguards. The venom of a snake was fearful but were there not herbs to counter it? Who though could explain the casting of a spell?[1] What power was this that could blurr the mind and glaze the eyes of its victim into vacant passivity? Who was it, who snatched the breath from a man's nostrils so that he moved no more? Who were the spirits who lived in swamp and tree and stone? Why were these demons so malignant and so hardly placated? Where would his own spirit flee at the last? What were the frontiers of the dark country beyond the darkness of the forest? Sulidan was old now, very old by the Dusun's reckoning. The time would not be long ere another sat where he sat and said to the people the things he said; and he would be but a memory and no more.

Many years before, there had come to live amongst the Dusuns of the Kota Belud district, a man of the white race. Such men from the unknown Western world were always a mystery to the tribal people. They seemed so few, their power so strong and their lives so selfish, but this man was different. His heart of care spoke from his eyes, and what is more he learned the tongue of the forest people. He spoke to them of the Great Spirit, of the Strong One, who made all things and was stronger than the strong. Over the years many turned to Christ and began to spread the news. One day a Dusun Christian met Sulidan and confronted him with the Gospel.

As he listened he knew that this was the Truth for which he had waited, that here, somehow, was the Answer to all his questionings and the Liberation from all his fears. He knew this was the turning point of his life, that he dare not return uncommitted, to the forest and its demons. With all the determination and faith that he knew he cast himself at the feet of Jesus Christ and confessed Him as his only Lord.

Sitting now in his hut the point was this, should he submit himself to men, as he had submitted himself to Christ? Hardly a day passed without men from the *kampongs* coming for his

[1] People actually die in Borneo, when under the terror of a curse or a spell. Authentic cases could be quoted.

advice and counsel. As they entered they submitted courteously to his authority and left to abide by the ruling which he gave, but now it was Sulidan's turn to go to others. No one else entered the hut that afternoon, so rising from his place he resolutely passed out of the shaded interior into the tropical sunshine. Eventually he came to Teginambur where devoted followers of his new-found Lord had already raised a leafy structure for a chapel, and where he could speak to those in Christ before him. What would they think about him? Soon he was sitting before the deacons, as those who were learning to take responsibility in the Church were called. Social status, local authority, the outward dignities of a chieftain were all laid aside. In the fellowship of the Church there is a submission to the Supreme Authority, to Christ who is Lord of all and Head over all. They listened to his personal testimony, and heard of the deliverance he had experienced, since believing in the Lord Jesus Christ. Slowly they weighed the evidence and asked their questions. Sulidan, their brother, patiently waited for their verdict. At last it came. "We are willing," they said, "for you to be baptised."

Did the Kadamayan ever run so clearly as that day when Sulidan stepped carefully down over the boulders into the cool, flowing waters to await his looked-for moment? Did Kinabalu ever stand in such splendour against the sky as that day, when Salidan obeyed his Lord's command? "Lord, by Thy favour Thou hast made my mountain to stand strong . . . Thy perfect love has cast out fear." So beneath the waters he passed in the Name of the Triune God. As he was helped from the river he eventually moved over to the stony water-course and sat there with the other Christians to pray. Suddenly in the stillness of the valley the cracked old lips of the converted chieftain burst into a pæan of thanksgiving. How often he had lisped and muttered the empty doggerel of the charms. Now his voice rang out in the pure bliss of worship, sounding the high praises of His great Redeemer. Higher and higher his voice ascended until those who witnessed this great outpouring of a 'young' believer's heart were moved to tears. Some may have wondered, perhaps, at so strong a demonstration of emotion from old Sulidan—but his song was the song of a man set free. Sulidan had been made anew.

The long sultry hours of the afternoon quickly passed and soon the sun was going down over the western jungle. Sulidan could not drag himself away. The new mystery of fellowship in Christ was filling him with wonder. Following the baptism he had sat with many others at the table of the Lord. How strangely satisfying it had all been to him. To be a chief was as nothing compared with being a son. On the table the ball of rice of which they had each partaken spoke so simply to him of the Saviour's body given for his sins. (The mode of observance conveyed no strangeness to Sulidan for they hardly know of bread in Dusun country.) Then, too, the juice of the coconut, how it had spoken of his Saviour's blood outpoured. (For him there was no straining of the Scripture for where the Dusuns live they have no other wine.) Thus in simplicity he had feasted and adored, and now he must face the lonely track and tread the two miles home. As he left, it was pitch black. It was his test of faith. Let the night be filled with demons and the forest echo with eerie calls of the unseen world! In his heart was the Stronger than the strong. There was no fear in love. Step by step he moved forward. Sulidan was conqueror. He knew he was doing what few Dusuns could do, but he would do it through Christ his Strength.

Eight months elapsed, then one day as he was sitting in his hut again, in came a messenger. The man, who looked tired after his long journey, handed the chieftain a little package carefully wrapped in broad green leaves, already turning brown. A few brief questions and Sulidan knew immediately that the carrier was from the Bandau country, fifty miles deeper in the interior. From the small leafy parcel, Sulidan eventually extricated a letter. He opened it, and scanned it, obviously finding very real difficulty in deciphering it, for he was not very good at reading in Malay. The following was the substance of the request which the unexpected letter contained.

"We have heard that you Sulidan, the chieftain, have become a Christian. All our village here are perplexed as to the true way to live, and concerning the right things to believe. We think our idols and our customs need to be changed. Are they not our ruin? What kind of Christianity is yours? Can you not come to us brother, and tell us of your faith?

"With Salutations,

"Your sister . . . of Tegare, Bandau."

As Sulidan folded the letter he knew what he would do. Of course, the journey was considerable but he *must* tell them. Just two or three days later the old man with his wife and their son, a youth in his twenties, set out along the trail for the Bandau country. The way was hot and the atmosphere humid. There were long stretches of jungle and leeches in the undergrowth. Snakes rustled into the bush. They waded through streams and clambered up and down the trail pouring with perspiration, their entire bodies strained and exhausted at the end of each day. On the third or fourth day they stumbled into the distant *kampong* and enquired for the home of Sulidan's sister. As she greeted him, she looked at him almost excitedly. It had been years since they had met and now Sulidan had not failed. He had answered their call.

Once refreshed Sulidan began to speak. How little he knew of Christian doctrine. How hopeless and inadequate he felt for the task of representing the Most High God to these, his fellow countrymen, who were as ignorant as he had been just a year ago. But he spoke what he knew and one can give no more eloquent a sermon than that. After a few days talking, the miracle suddenly happened. Certain people began removing the idols and the charms from their houses. There was a deep stirring in the *kampong*. Sulidan watched with wonder. This was *his* God at work. In the Name of Jesus the very demons that he used to serve were falling as he preached. In all, three families abandoned idolatry in favour of the Christian 'customs'. Others also said they would 'follow' but did this mean they were really turning to Christ? Had they understood who Jesus was? Or what He had done for them? Sulidan was perplexed. He knew not how to go on. Cast upon God he decided he must return to Teginambur and get help from those more experienced in the Faith than he. Thus, after only a short while in Bandau, he returned, accompanied by one or two who were yearning after the true God.

The very first Sunday he was back in Teginambur he stood up before the assembled church and made his report, uttering an impassioned plea, for helpers to go at once to Bandau. 'The harvest was white', the people were turning, they waited now for more news of the Saviour. He had told them what he could. Would no one return with him to Bandau? The old man's voice died away in the leafy chapel—but no one moved. How could they go? There was so much to be done in the fields. Their own village must work to eat. How could any of the men be spared? —so the call went unanswered. Sulidan, sad at heart, said nothing. He had not returned to Teginambur to criticise and anyway he was just a babe in Christ. Perhaps others knew better than he, but for himself he was sure the work at Bandau must go on. Some few days later there was a whisper going from hut to hut. "Have you heard the news? They say the old chieftain is moving out of the village to go and live permanently at Bandau? You can hardly believe it. You would think a man of his years and influence would have more sense. The spirits will retaliate without a doubt—deserting the village of his ancestors like that. They say, too, it's all to do with this Jesus doctrine!" Thus gradually the news spread and a great astonishment arose in the community, but Sulidan departed, caring little for the atmosphere of amazement he was leaving behind.

Once it was known that Sulidan had come to live in Tegare[1] and that he was no longer just a visitor but a resident, the headman of the Bandau district became perturbed. What were the motives of this ex-chieftain taking up abode in his area? It was not long before this headman, an ardent Moslem, came to realise that there was an aggressive Christian witness expanding in the

[1] Tegare, a village in the Bandau district.

territory under his jurisdiction. Sulidan now began to meet his severest opposition. Every attempt was made to extradite him but in as much as many years ago he had been permitted to live there a short while, a precedent had been established and it was impossible to endorse such an order with any legal authority. In spite of such official hostility Sulidan stood his ground and through sheer determination of faith, weathered the storm to continue his work of witnessing to Christ. One year, two years, three years passed. It had been hard but now there were twenty-five definite believers in the Lord Jesus Christ in Bandau. Surely the time had come to return to Teginambur and once again ask for a Bible Teacher to come and establish the work.

Sulidan, now well into his sixties, took the trail again. As evidence of the fruit of his labours two converts accompanied him adding weight to his plea. They desired to be baptised and Salidan decided to take them to the church at Teginambur and from thence to the Kadamayan river. What memories rose within the old man as he watched these two young believers from Bandau stand where he stood those years before and go down into the waters of the river. Again he knew that he was doing what no mere man could do. God was working through him to the salvation of his people, some of whom he himself once ruled, but could never have saved from sin and fear. When Sulidan stood this second time under the leafy roof of the Teginambur chapel, he was full of hope. He told of the developments, of the opposition, and yet of the triumphs of God. Would no one come? He could hardly believe there was no response. As a chieftain, everyone had obeyed him without question. Now he spoke as a Christian to Christians, but nobody seemed to care what he said. Again he added nothing, but with that same earlier determination possessing him, and fortified with a growing spiritual maturity, he set his face once more to the task.

On arriving back in Bandau he re-doubled his efforts, willing to spend the very last days of his life wholly for his Lord. The demands on him were tremendous. In the following six months, the breath of God swept through the little *kampong*. From twenty-five, the number of believers grew to ninety. They built their own leaf shelter for their meetings. How could he teach them, a deaf old man failing in strength, with no Bible in the Dusun tongue and so poor a grasp of written Malay? His heart yearned to see these young believers established in Christ. Would nobody come to their aid? Would no one join hands with him and unfold to them the unsearchable riches of Christ?

With heart aflame the old man took his last fifty-mile journey back to Teginambur.

As he stood for the very last time in the leafy chapel[1] he was more frail than before. Perhaps his voice was not so strong—but the power of the Holy Spirit was with him. Who could withstand the call of God to go into the Bandau country? His request was large. "We want a missionary," the old man cried. "We want a Bible School. We want a Christian schoolteacher for the children." He was determined that the breach in the enemy's lines should be exploited to the full and that he might see the full overthrow of Satan in the district of Bandau. This was his vision. Sulidan did not wait for a response. He immediately returned to finish his work. Very soon it was Easter time in the year 1959 and in the strength of the Risen Saviour, one of the deacons of the church at Teginambur, together with a number of believers, decided to answer the call and reach out to Bandau. Their legs were younger and stronger than Salidan's and they made the journey without undue difficulty. Through the glades and into the open stretches of the *kampong* they came, their hearts rejoicing in the prospect of strengthening the hands of their aged brother and joining him in the work—but he was nowhere to be seen. They enquired for his home and found it—but all was strangely quiet. They mounted the steps of the crude hut and pushed open the door. On a rough mat in a darkened corner Sulidan lay very ill with pneumonia. There were few comforts. There was no medical aid. He had given all for the Kingdom. As Sulidan sensed the presence of his visitors he opened his eyes and recognised his friends and brothers from Teginambur. A

[1] Now enlarged to a semi-permanent building seating 1000.

light filled the tired and faded countenance. "I have been asking God," he said, "to let me see your faces ... and now you've come ... He's heard my prayer ... I am ready if He calls me now."

The evening shadows slanted down through the coconut palms and night fell once more over the distant jungle. The young men kept watch over Sulidan. The torch was being passed on. The light of the Gospel would not fail. God's own relief had come and now the old man slept.

The next day all was hushed in Sulidan's hut. No one spoke. It was the moment of a great departure. Men's eyes were too full of tears for words. Suddenly through all the heavens beyond the peak of Kinabalu, the sky was filled with trumpeting. There were those who heard it, and from the gloomy shadows of the tiny shack, Sulidan stepped into the presence of his King.

CHAPTER FIFTEEN

FAREWELL TO BORNEO

That I might finish my course with joy.   Paul

A VISIT to the shipping office in Jesselton confirmed that the S.S. *Kunak* would be arriving from Singapore on the following Wednesday. How the fourteen months had flown. Now the hours seemed all too few for the preparations of our departure and our friends' return. Over the steps leading down into the garden hung wire frames full of orchid plants. Each day found us examining that butterfly orchid. It had never bloomed before but now a slender purple stem was gradually protruding from the mass of leaves. Along the stem at regular intervals tiny brown buds like little clenched fists were beginning to unfold, relaxing their apparent tension. As we looked we were always wondering, "Will it bloom to welcome Mrs. Pucknell home." How she loved the flowers! How she had longed for England's daffodils in the heat of Borneo. If this one butterfly orchid could but burst forth in all its pure white radiance, it would be the loveliest welcome of all.

Then we looked at the flooring in the house. The feet and toys of two small boys had not improved it. Let's buy some lino! So we did, and amidst profuse perspiration managed to put it down. But what about the garden? Better have the little old man along once more. So to the sound and the 'tootle' of the rotary, not forgetting the blue haze of exhaust, the mangrove grass was clipped again. Then, of course, there was the landlord. Genial as ever, he kindly reproofed the mosquito netting even though the last rent was already paid.

Gradually the wardrobe and the drawers began to empty and our cases began to fill. We had come out with three! How did we ever do it? We must buy another one! Still not enough— and so another!

The day the Pucknells arrived we were down at the wharf about 8 a.m. and from then on there was a continual stream of Christians to the boat. Ta-Ko, Te-Ping, Ko-Ko, Chang-Shen, Nat and all the others had looked forward with us to this moment. Many had grown considerably in their spiritual lives during the past year and quite a number had been baptised. It was very moving for us all to meet again in the ship's lounge and rehearse the goodness of our God.

That evening the whole Church assembled in the little meeting hall, packing it to the doors until we could only sit the children on the tables. As brother Pucknell rose to speak there was close attention. Opening the Bible he read the telling words that expressed the deep longings of his heart.

"But we, brethren, being taken from you for a short time in presence, not in heart, endeavoured the more abundantly to see your face with great desire . . . And having this confidence, I know that I shall abide and continue with you all for your furtherance and joy of faith."[1]

For more than thirty years he had laboured amongst the Chinese people and now, although more than sixty, he was turning his face again into the wind, and bending his back once more to the burden. The responsibility lay heavily upon him, but the God of yesterday would be all-sufficent for the morrow, thus on this day of his return he could speak to them, trusting the fullness of God's Grace . . .

So to the final morning . . . As we awoke and gathered up our last-minute bits-and-pieces, the storm clouds overhead began to recede, and by the time we were driving to the airport the sky was brightening fast. Many who had welcomed us were there to say farewell. Some came with their gifts. There was a bag of oranges, a box of chocolates, tins of biscuits, toys for the children, a Dusun hat, a length of cloth and even money from those very close to us. Finally, there was an envelope containing a love-gift from the Church. So many 'thank yous', so many handshakes and so few moments when it came to it, to say good-bye. It was

[1] I Thessalonians 2, v. 17 and Philippians 1, v. 25.

hard to mix the smiles and tears as the announcement of our flight boomed out over the loudspeakers. An airport official pulled the iron gates roughly back and we walked out across the tarmac. A little sixteen-seater 'twin-pioneer' was waiting for us and as we clambered up the metal steps we could hear the Christians singing on the airport balcony. The breeze veered in our direction and we caught the words. How good it was to hear them.

> "On the victory side,
> On the victory side!
> With Christ within,
> The fight we'll win,
> On the victory side!"

A last wave and the door was slammed. Just a short taxying into position and then the little plane rose steeply into the southern sky. Once again we were over the jungle and looking down on the surf-washed shore. Once again we glimpsed the mangroves and the green, green hills. Slowly the tiny offshore islands merged in the horizon.

This time it was good-bye to Borneo. A change of planes at Brunei, and by evening we would be coasting in along the great runway of the Hong Kong harbour.

Suddenly a little voice piped up. "Where's the man that brings the food?" It was Ross. "We're standing still," says Peter, looking into outer space. But no, we were moving on. In Christ's great service the will of God must always be obeyed. Another task was waiting to be done.

THE LAND—ITS PROFILE AND ITS PEOPLES

(General notes on British North Borneo suitable for
Missionary Study Classes etc.)

Physical Features

BRITISH NORTH BORNEO comprises the more northerly and
western extremities of the great island of Borneo. The territory,
which is reminiscent of an equilateral triangle, denuded at its
base angles, has an area of 29,388 square miles and lies between
the latitudes of 4 and 7 degrees north and the longitudes of 115
and 119 degrees east. It is thus wholly situated in the torrid
zone.

The colony is contiguous with Sarawak and Kalimantan, the
latter being that part of the island administered by the Indonesian
Republic. North Borneo, Sarawak and Brunei, the other state
in the island, are all politically associated with Great Britain. To
anyone living in North Borneo there is often a sense of remote-
ness, and this is in measure understandable, as the China coast is
some 1200 miles away to the north and the Australian coast
some 1500 miles to the south.

The northern tip of the colony's territory is guarded by the
islands, Balembangan and Banggi. It is here that the coastline of
the colony is divided into the conventional terms of east coast
and west coast, whilst just to the north the Balabac Strait marks
the link between the Sulu and the South China Seas. The more
southerly flank of the east coast, however, is bounded by the
Celebes Sea. One of the special features of the coastline is found
in the numerous coral reefs and islands, dangerous to shipping
but inviting to smaller craft. They are frequently uninhabited,
covered with jungle, but serve as a base for native fishermen. Of
these islands, Labuan perhaps is an exception, having upon it the
town of Victoria and a sizeable airfield. North Borneo has some

fine beaches, but much of the shore in places is a maze of mangrove swamps.

Dominating the North Borneo landscape is the impressive ridge-like peak of Mount Kinabalu. It rises 13,455 feet above sea level and is by far the most outstanding peak of the Crocker Range, which commences near the Sarawak border in the south and runs northward through practically the entire length of the country. The average height of the ridges is somewhere between 2500 and 4000 feet. The range keeps fairly parallel to the west coast, mostly between twenty and fifty miles from the sea. East of the Crocker Range lie the Witti and Maitland Ranges, and in the northern part of this latter system we have the second highest peak in the colony, namely Mount Trus Madi, rising 8500 feet above sea level.

The most well known of the plains are the west coast plain and the Tambunan plain, both of which are quite extensively cultivated. There is also the Keningau plain which until recently was scrub and grassland but is now being extensively developed. Apart from these breaks in the forest growth the whole interior, right away south to the Indonesian border, is jungle ridden, mountainous and still largely unfrequented. This applies also to much of the interior of the eastern portion of the territory. Timber and ore prospectors, however, do go in and different groups of surveyors undertake exploratory itinerations.

To fly over Borneo gives some idea of the great watersheds. Flowing eastward from the Witti Range is the largest river in the colony, called the Kinabatangan. It is 350 miles long and enters the sea between Sandakan and Tambisan. Other rivers worthy of mention are the Segama, the Sugut and the Labuk. On the west coast the only river of note is the Padas. Most rivers of the west are fast flowing and not so navigable as those of the east. In many places in the interior rivers provide the sole means of communication between one place and another, and with the growing supply of outboard motors, canoes are giving way to launches.

Climate

This represents the biggest single factor of hardship for the European working in North Borneo. The climate is equatorial in every sense of the word. Most days the temperature runs between 80 and 86 degrees. Nights can be equally hot but on occasions there is a drop, sometimes to as low as 74 degrees. Without air conditioning, room temperatures tend to reach 90 to 94 degrees. The difficult aspect of the climate lies in its being so equable and so humid. The scarcity of hill-stations and mountain resorts, means that it becomes inescapable for most people. The Ranau rest-house at 2000 feet is probably the only real hill-station in the colony, although Keningau at 600 feet can give some cooler nights.

Rainfall is heavy, being as much as 160 inches a year in places.

During May and August there is the southwest Monsoon bringing the west coast its heaviest rainfall. Then between November and April the northeast Monsoon blows to bring the east coast its heaviest rainfall. Rainstorms can be very severe with high winds and vehement squalls, bending the palm trees low and doubling back their fronds to resemble inverted umbrellas, but the colony is spared the havoc of the big typhoons as it lies just south of the typhoon belt.

Population

The 1960 census revealed a registered population of almost 455,000 persons. Of this number the biggest tribal group proved to be the Dusuns (or Kadazans). The word Dusun is not used by the natives themselves as it is a term banding together quite a number of similar tribes. This group is physically small, pleasantly featured, sallow-brown as to skin, with black hair and bright eyes. They are hard working, have adapted themselves well to agriculture and are a friendly people. Then there are 22,000 Muruts. This tribe appears to be still more primitive and perhaps less industrious than the Dusuns. Only a generation or two ago they were head-hunters, and you can still see shrivelled skulls hanging in some of their older buildings in the jungle interior. Their facial expression seems harsher and less relaxed than the Dusuns. If anything they are of even smaller build and are more of a pigmy race, who originally lived in the gloom of the rain forests. Up till the 1951 census the Murut population continued to decline, but the 1960 census is encouraging, showing an increase of over 3000 in the last ten years.

Over on the east coast live the Bajaus. These are a sea-loving native people populating not only parts of Borneo but also some of the islands of the Philippine archipelago. They share with the Illanus, Saluks, Obians, Binadans and other smaller tribal groups, the reputation of being descendants of the pirates that were so constant a menace in earlier years to the development of trade.

Other groups that should be mentioned are the Bruneis and the Kedayans. There are between twenty and thirty thousand of these people. They are mostly fishermen and are found largely on the west coast. There are also various Indian nationalities.

The biggest single group alien to the island of Borneo is the Chinese. It will surprise some readers to know that there are 105,000 Chinese in North Borneo alone. This is sufficient for them to change practically every town in the colony into a little Chinatown. They control much of the commerce, fill the higher centres of education and occupy many an important post. Most are glad to be in Borneo and they contribute loyally to the general well-being of the colony. With Communist China, however, to the north, it is inevitable that in so large a number of persons there will be those who will give themselves to subversive activity and the presence of so many Chinese will undoubtedly become a growing embarrassment to the administration as Communist infiltration increases in S.E. Asia.

There are two to three thousand Eurasians, but Europeans number only a few hundred. The white community is thus very limited and entry of Europeans to the colony is restricted to those who go either for a short visit, or for purposes sanctioned by the Government. Even in these circumstances it is necessary for the entrant to have a guarantor in the colony willing to put down a deposit or, alternatively, to be officially sponsored by a reputable business house or organisation in his own country. Most Europeans in the colony are there on Government appointments.

The population is thus made up of many races. Malaya being the nearest Commonwealth neighbour and there being historical links with the former British administration of the Malayan Federation, the Malay language is the *lingua franca* and the same currency is still used in both Malaya and North Borneo.

Produce

A land that is largely covered by equatorial forest and dense jungle is bound to have a good deal of natural products coming from these great reserves. Timber is therefore one of the main exports from North Borneo, together with minor forest produce such as firewood, charcoal, cutch, damar, nuts, etc. Amongst the more remunerative, however, must rank rubber, copra and tobacco. Rubber and coconut plantations are extensive in the plains and whilst not so orderly, or operated on the same scale as those in Malaya, they are nevertheless quite large. In the southeast part of the colony hemp is being grown for export. There is also a certain amount of dried and salted fish sent abroad. Coffee is an increasing export and the cocoa crop is rising. A new venture is the introduction of the oil palm. This is now being planted on a fair scale and beginning to create an income. Crops for more local consumption include, first of all, rice. (There are quite a lot of paddy fields to be seen as one moves about the coastal plain.) Then there are crops like maize, groundnuts and soya beans, and experiments are being tried in other possible production.

In North Borneo, up till now, there is no heavy industry. There are deposits of coal, iron and some chromite but nothing is being mined on a commercial scale except limestone, sand and the coral being extracted for purely local purposes.

Wild Life

Whilst the vegetation of Borneo is very luxuriant to the casual observer the countryside seems strangely devoid of life. There is something almost deathly as you walk through the silence and darkness of the forest. In this sense North Borneo is disappointing. There are, nevertheless, numerous animals hiding from view and the patient naturalist is rewarded by glimpses of them.

The most numerous of the animals of North Borneo are the apes and monkeys which include the gibbon, the orang-utan and the diminutive tarsier. There is also the musang, a furry creature with beady eyes, long tail and in size somewhat bigger than a cat. There are estimated to be a few hundred elephants but these are hardly indigenous and are reputed to have been originally introduced from India.

Wild pig is a favourite target for the hunter, and forages in the plantations and along the rivers. Other animals are the honey-bear, the scaly ant-eater and various kinds of deer. Birds are for the most part small and few in numbers, and one tends to miss them but there are exceptions such as the magnificent rhinoceros hornbill.

Amongst the reptiles there are numerous snakes but few are poisonous. Crocodiles and iguanas frequent the rivers and marshes. Insect life is sometimes quite spectacular to the visitor from temperate climates. Gigantic moths, beautiful butterflies and the dreaded centipedes, together with the bulbous bumble bees, quickly claim attention. Mosquitoes, some malarial, are still a plague, but the authorities have done much to reduce the incidence of malaria amongst the people.

Communications

These are still limited and for the most part primitive, there being barely 300 miles of properly made-up road in the colony. There are, however, nearly a thousand miles of gravel tracks and bridle paths.

Thus the main link between major centres is by air, and there are regular services linking Jesselton, the capital, with Labuan, Sandakan, Ranau, Keningau, Lahad Datu, Tawau and Kudat. Labuan has the potential of being an international airport and at times links North Borneo with Singapore, Hong

Kong, Indonesia and Australia, although most airlines use Brunei for this purpose.

Certain shipping lines also link the main ports such as Jesselton, Labuan, Kudat, Sandakan, Tawau, Lahad Datu and Semporna. There is a short railway on the west coast.

Travel in the deep interior is limited to local footpaths or river transport.

History

Magellan is usually considered to be the discoverer of Borneo. That was in 1521 when he called at Brunei on one of his great voyages, and this date is viewed as the first reliable reference to the country in more modern history.

The Chinese, however, had contact with Borneo from antiquity. Such accounts go back as far as the Sung dynasty (A.D. 960–1279), but how reliable they are is difficult to say. Considering, however, the proximity of Borneo to China, it is highly probable that the Chinese visited Borneo over a thousand years ago. Some historians mention that the Chinese stationed officials on the island even earlier. In the fourteenth century the Mongol conquerors are said to have landed in Borneo and in the fifteenth century one of the Ming emperors, named Yun Lo, sent an expedition to the territory.

It was only in the sixteenth century that the European appeared on the scene, beginning with the Portuguese, who were followed in turn by the Spanish, the Dutch and finally the British.

In 1882, the British North Borneo Chartered Company was formed with authority to administer North Borneo, and in May 1888, North Borneo, together with Brunei and Sarawak, became a British Protectorate. The term of the Charter authorised the company to administer justice in North Borneo with due regard to native law and the prevailing customs; to abolish slavery and to maintain a policy of non-interference with the religion of the natives.

This company undertook these responsibilities for the British

Crown until 1942 when Japanese troops landed, overthrew the authority and occupied the territory until 1945. In that year Australian units liberated the country and the territory reverted to the British. In 1946, North Borneo was proclaimed a Crown Colony and the Colonial Office became responsible for its administration.

Administration

At the time of writing the administration remains largely colonial in character, the country still being a British Crown Colony. Up to the spring of 1961, there was still no elected parliament but political parties had already emerged and plans for the electing of local authorities were in preparation. Thus big constitutional changes are imminent. The suggestion recently put forward by the Prime Minister of Malaya, Tengku Abdul Rahman, for a Greater Malaysia, which would bring the Borneo territories of British connection into federation with Malaya and Singapore, has been acclaimed in many quarters as a wise political proposal. Should these plans be implemented, they will undoubtedly prove a decisive factor in determining the future constitution of North Borneo. Meanwhile the head of the administration in the colony is a British Government officer bearing the title, 'Governor and Commander-in-Chief'.

Routine administration throughout the colony is superintended by departments under the general direction of the Chief Secretary, who is the principal executive officer of the Government.

Regional administration is carried out by dividing the colony into four regions called 'Residencies'. These are the West Coast Residency, the Sandakan Residency, the Interior Residency and the Tawau Residency. The Chief Officer of each Residency is a person holding the title of 'The Resident'. Under him are several districts each with a District Officer and under the District Officers are the native chiefs and village headmen, each with their prescribed authority.

Approach to local government authority is through the

District Officer, whilst approach to higher government authorities is through the Resident.

Religion

Most of the major tribal groups are animists, worshipping and dreading spirits, ghosts and demons, whom they believe inhabit the trees, the hills and the rivers. Amongst the coastal communities, however, quite a proportion of the people are Moslems.

The Chinese for the most part hold vaguely to a Confucian ethic but are bound far more firmly by the trappings and superstitions attending a corrupted Buddhism. There is a little Hinduism, there being a small but quite definite Indian community. The Sikhs have a temple on the outskirts of Jesselton.

Those professing Christianity, that is as a religion distinct from other faiths in the colony, are rated as numerous as 60,000. Of these, 36,000 are Dusun, 5,000 Murut and 24,000 Chinese. Amongst these, many would be persons with only the merest and most nominal connections with Roman Catholicism, Seventh Day Adventism, etc. For all the apparently large numbers who might state Christianity as their faith, it is still difficult to find very many who will confess the Lord Jesus Christ as their personal Saviour.

The history of foreign missions goes back at least a hundred years. The Roman Catholics and the Anglican Society for the Propagation of the Gospel have the most longstanding work in the colony, the latter coming to the country over a century ago. This latter group is high church in its approach and has established churches and schools in most of the larger towns. At Tawau, however, the Anglican Mission is evangelical and is staffed by Australians. The Anglican work is chiefly amongst the Chinese and the Dusuns. Their emphasis on schools has provided many a young person in Borneo with the opportunity of receiving a secondary school education.

The Seventh Day Adventists came later but have nevertheless been active in the colony for about sixty years. Their roots are deep and their work extensive.

Another group of some fifteen to twenty churches is that of the Basel Mission, operated by Chinese pastors and mainly Lutheran in outlook. These people work amongst the Hakka-speaking Chinese.

The Hakkas are the largest group of Chinese-speaking peoples in the colony. Many of them came from China about half a century ago, whilst others have been recruited over the years, generally to take part in government-sponsored agricultural schemes. Numbers of the recruits were professing Christians from the work of the Basel Mission in S.E. China. They brought no foreign missionary with them but were accompanied by some of their own native pastors. Once in Borneo they soon erected buildings which served as schools on week-days and places of worship on Sundays. Later, separate church buildings were built. Today there are still some evangelicals witnessing amongst them.

Just over fifteen years ago an inter-denominational evangelical mission which had its field headquarters in Sarawak, obtained permission to work in North Borneo amongst the Muruts and the Dusuns. This is known as the Borneo Evangelical Mission. Most of their workers come from Australia. Showing outstanding devotion to Christ they worked fearlessly amongst the primitive people of the interior, who at that time had been left largely to their own devices, because of their anti-social tendencies. The Mission opened up stations and settlements far away in the forests, organised the construction of landing strips, and with their little single-engined monoplanes put in teachers, doctors, nurses and others to meet the challenge of heathen darkness and disease.

With the Bible, new kinds of seeds, medicines, clothes, etc., these pagan people had every part of their life changed for the better, and today in many places in North Borneo and Sarawak, where the natives were previously roaming about with just loin cloths and blow-pipes, suffering from malnutrition, and decimating themselves with such evil practices as head-hunting, there are now healthily settled communities with flourishing crops. The greatest triumph of all, however, is that many of these people are truly converted to God and have a deep love for the Lord Jesus Christ, that sends them out preaching His Gospel to others who have not yet heard His Name.

Outstanding work is also being done amongst tribal peoples by the Teginambur Christian Fellowship (see Chapter 14), and other evangelical workers.

In about 1950 evangelical missionaries from Great Britain who had originally worked with assemblies of Christians in Central China prior to the Communist advance, visited North Borneo. Following a time of survey they eventually obtained permission to work amongst the Chinese- and English-speaking peoples of Tanjong Aru, Jesselton and the district of Tenom. These missionaries were Mr. and Mrs. F. W. Puckell and Mr. and Mrs. George Hanlon. In the short history of the work some five churches have been founded, two in Tanjong Aru, where there are about eighty believers in church fellowship, and three in the Tenom area, where some seventy have been baptised during the last four years, 1957-61. Within the last year official permission has been granted for extending the work amongst other Chinese communities of the West Coast Residency, and progress has already been made in the townships of Kota Belud and Keningau.

This work is in Mandarin, Hakka and English. Whilst mostly devoted to the work of preaching, other aspects of the venture which have proved fruitful are the Emmans Bible School correspondence course work and the agency of the Bible Societies in Malaya opened in Jesselton by Mr. Pucknell. In later years they have been joined by Mr. and Mrs. David Smith, Mr. and Mrs. Boyd Aitken and Miss Joyce Shackley. The author served for some fourteen and a half months in Borneo, in this missionary connection.

'Coral in the Sand' is a true-life story. Apart from the slight alteration of a few details here and there, and the introduction of alternative names for some local characters, it is a factual record. That these things really happened is part of the essential challenge of the book.

Bibliography

The North Borneo Annual Reports, obtainable from H.M. Stationery Office.

Under Chartered Company Rule; North Borneo 1881–1946, by K. G. Tregonning. Singapore, University of Malaya Press, 1958.

North Borneo, by K. G. Tregonning.

The Religion of the Tempasuk Dusuns of North Borneo, by I. H. N. Evans. Cambridge University Press, 1952.

Land Below the Wind, by Agnes Keith. Michael Joseph, 1939.

Three Came Home, by Agnes Keith. Michael Joseph, 1955.

A Bibliography of Malaya; also a short list of books relating to North Borneo and Sarawak. Kuala Lumpur, 1939.

A Tragedy of Borneo 1941–45. Kinabalu National Memorial Park Project brochure.

Sabah Story. A Guide Book issued by the Rotary Club of Jesselton, North Borneo.

Information Pamphlet on North Borneo, published by Royal Commonwealth Society, London.

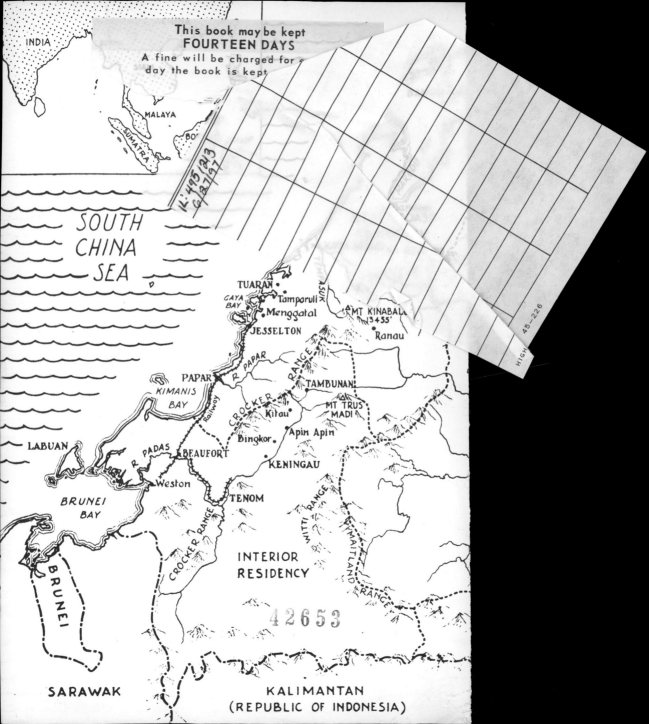

INDIA

MALAYA

SUMATRA

BO

SOUTH
CHINA
SEA

TUARAN
GAYA
BAY
Tamparuli
Menggatal
MT KINABALU
3455'
JESSELTON
Ranau
R PAPAR
PAPAR
KIMANIS
BAY
CROCKER RANGE
Railway
Kitau
TAMBUNAN
MT TRUS
MADI
LABUAN
Bingkor
Apin Apin
R PADAS
BEAUFORT
KENINGAU
Weston
BRUNEI
BAY
TENOM
CROCKER RANGE
WITTI RANGE
MAITLAND RANGE
BRUNEI
INTERIOR
RESIDENCY

42653

SARAWAK
KALIMANTAN
(REPUBLIC OF INDONESIA)